MESHULLAM!

OR, TIDINGS

FROM JERUSALEM.

FROM THE JOURNAL OF

A BELIEVER

RECENTLY RETURNED FROM THE

HOLY LAND.

Comfort ye—comfort ye, my people,
Saith your God—speak ye comfortably,
To Jerusalem and CRY unto her,
That her welfare is accomplished.—*Isa.* xl. 1, 2

SECOND EDITION, REVISED:
PUBLISHED BY THE AUTHOR
1851.

MESHULLAM!

OR, TIDINGS

FROM JERUSALEM.

FROM THE JOURNAL OF

A BELIEVER

RECENTLY RETURNED FROM THE

HOLY LAND.

Comfort ye—comfort ye, my people,
Saith your God—speak ye comfortably,
To Jerusalem and CRY unto her,
That her welfare is accomplished.—*Isa.* xl. 1, 2.

SECOND EDITION, REVISED:
PUBLISHED BY THE AUTHOR.
1851.

JOHN C. ROBB, PRINTER, 8 Pear Street, Philadelphia.

R. P. MOGRIDGE, STEREOTYPER, Franklin Place.

APOLOGY
FOR THE SECOND EDITION.

The unexpected clemency and approbation which the first edition of this little work has received from the public press—Secular, Literary, and Religious,—in this city and elsewhere, the deep interest in its subject, awakened in the hearts of many devoted and inquiring Christians, and the increasing demands for copies, must be our first apology for the present reprint of the "Tidings from Jerusalem." We are happy to add the independent testimony of different individuals,—in Germany and Palestine, who are interested and engaged in the same object, in confirmation of the positions and facts already given. We also give extracts from another letter from Mr. Meshullam, his wife, and eldest son, with his receipt of the first donations from this land to aid his work in *Bethlehem*.

Three months have passed since "the Tidings" were published. One thousand copies by an obscure individual effort, have been widely scattered, and returns for half its printing received. But for Jerusalem's sake we cannot rest, and again send forth our weak appeal, in behalf of the mourners and ashes of Zion. We bring facts well attested, a providential opportunity for active Christian benevolence, unparalleled!

But who will believe our report, and faithfully respond to its call! *An intelligent devoted Israelite in* BETHLEHEM, *has successfully commenced the cultivation of the desolate soil!* He proposes to extend his labors, and teach his suffering brethren, this first true art of livelihood! He writes that he cannot receive the applications which they make. He appeals to us for aid, not for himself, but for the destitute and dying! the devout remnant of Israel, who are imprisoned by want, among the ruins of Jerusalem! Where are the professed friends of the natural seed of Abraham? Many professions of love have been written and spoken, but where is the reality? the "MERCY" by which "they may find mercy." A few laboring and devoted Christians are ready to go and co-operate with him, and sacrifice their life to this object, to cultivate and build the desolate wastes, and comfort the captive daughter of Jerusalem! THEY WAIT,—and the responsibility of their delay rests not at their humble thresholds.*

If Meshullam should fail in his noble beginning, and his hands hang down with his unrelieved burden, how shall we meet the crucified and COMING ONE, when he shall say, I was an hungered,—I was thirsty,—I was a stranger,—naked,—sick,—and in prison,—and ye ministered not unto me in these my NATURAL brethren.

A moderate, economical expenditure is all that is needful to begin the work, which, with the Divine blessing on judicious manual labor, will soon sustain itself, and extend its aid to many destitute Jewish families. As I close these last pencilings—the cold certainty comes over my heart that many a professed lover of Jesus will pass by on the other side, and leave this humble work, and its blessing to some poor Samaritan, and retire to their "ceiled houses," while the place of the name of the Lord of Hosts lies desolate.

* See Appeal at close of the volume.

PHILADELPHIA, March 28, 1851.

INTRODUCTION.

THROUGH the solicitation of some dear Christian friends in England, and in Philadelphia, and with a humble hope of encouraging some of the weakest of "the household of FAITH," I have been led to publish this imperfect journal, which at first was hastily pencilled by the way, and was only designed for the eye of one or two beloved friends in Christ, whose kind sympathy and aid has long been used of the Lord, as a strength and solace, in the trying walk of faith.

From my earliest recollections, through the influence of a devoted and praying mother, (whom I lost at an early age,) I have, with more or less desire, been seeking to KNOW and serve the living God. Many failures, at different times, have humbled and chastened my soul before him. Twenty-four years I was conscientiously walking in connexion with the Congregational Church of a Puritan ancestry, and, with little sectarianism, cherished attachment and reverence, for the ministry and churches of all evangelical Protestanism. I had entire confidence in the Scriptures, and received their most literal and definite sense in regard to present, practical duty, and future promise. In the latter part of these years, I began to realize a great discrepancy between the religion and form of godliness in this age, and its power manifested in the Scriptures in the lives of its early witnesses. This caused my heart much grief and discouragement, as to our common salvation. I searched commentaries, and read the biographies of ancient and later Christian experience, which more confirmed my sense of the great degeneracy of our common profession of religion, in its general falling away, coldness of love, and weakness of spiritual life. This mostly I realized in myself, and often struggled, with fastings and tears, for a greater nearness to the life of Christ, knowing that no corporate, or general failure, is any excuse for individual unfaithfulness. I felt a sincere sympathy for all benevolent effort, and according to means and opportunity, I sought to relieve my need of spirit by such active service. In this course, I sometimes experienced the Divine presence, and blessing, but felt a want of life and sufficiency in all outward means, and became still more and more dissatisfied with my low state of spiritual attainment. I studied with interest the unfulfilled portions of the prophetic Scriptures, relating to the New Earth and a state of blessedness in the dim future. In this state of mind, in the autumn of 1842, I first heard the Gospel, of "the kingdom of God at hand," and the pre-millenial advent of our blessed Lord and Saviour Jesus Christ!

It was a startling sound, as a thrilling melody from heaven, awaking my soul from its pale dreams of midnight, to their certain, near and more glorious reality. At first I dared not believe, and commenced a new search of the prophetic word, with a life and dilligence unkown before, accompanied with sincere humiliation and earnest cries to God for his help and guidance. After some weeks of intense application, the Lord in great mercy began to open my understanding, with deep convictions of its reality, to see and receive his truth. I cannot here speak of the searching, santifying experience, that followed of strivings, and tears, and prayers, for a preparation to meet the Lord, and to be accepted of him, and of the inward *life*, and joy unspeakable succeeding,—for my belief in the nearness of the *time* of his coming, made my case imperative. True, I then only apprehended *some* of the great outlines of the prophetic chart, for with many fundamental points of truth, were mixed serious misapprehensions and remains of tradition, which since, I humbly trust, have been mostly removed. *This* long-neglected truth, of the personal coming, and reign of Christ, which was the life, and "blessed hope," of the New Testament ministry in the first call of the Gentiles in the East, began to be truly revived in Germany and in England during the last fifty years, and afterwards, about the year 1843, it burst forth in its closing power in this far Western land, of the setting sun. Such was its power, that the sound echoed through the extent of Christendom, and many of us believed, as did the disciples when Jesus rode in Jerusalem, that "the kingdom would immediately appear." But we *now* see that "the day of his preparation," must precede his coming, and in this "TIME of the END many shall be purified, and made white, and tried," and have an understanding of the times, while the wicked are doing wickedly, and do not understand. It is represented as a short time, when "the just shall live by faith," and have need of patience, that they may ENDURE unto the end. It is "the day of (or preceding) his coming," which few can abide, for "he is like a refiner's fire, and fuller's soap," when his fan is in his hand, and he will thoroughly purge his floor," that He may "gather the wheat into his garner," at his appearing; the "perilous times," of the last days of the times of the Gentiles," when righteousness must greatly decline, and fall away, and "men shall be lovers of their own selves," *and have the form* and profession of godliness, and deny its *power;* "the days of the Son of Man," which are as "the days of Noah and Lot," on account of great wickedness, preceding sudden judgment, when the SON OF MAN SHALL COME, and a king shall reign in righteousness," upon Mount Zion, and the Lord shall be king over all the earth." Then shall come "the regeneration, when the Son of Man shall sit on the throne of his glory," and bring the "restitution of all things, which God hath spoken, by the mouth of all his holy prophets since the world began;" when the promise of Abraham will be fulfilled, to all his natural and spiritual seed, and the curse of the *land* shall be removed, and it shall become "as the garden of the Lord." As the experiment of disobedience, and sin, through the first Adam, has been fully wrought in six thousand years of misery and death, so now, the redemption through the grace of Jesus Christ, the second Adam, will be gloriously shown, and finished, in his personal reign, with his saints, for one thousand years, "for he must reign, till he hath put all enemies under his feet." In that time, all things shall be subdued unto him, after which the kingdom shall be delivered up unto the Father, and God shall be all in all, in the final glory of the New Jerusalem.

Many can now unite, in something like this general outline, of the hope of the Scriptures; but there seems to be a twilight as to DISTINCT vision, in most believing minds, overshadowing, and confusing the events, that directly unite the present and future dispensation, and usher in the MOMENT of the Lord's coming. Consequently, a great variety of expectations exist, as to the immediate future. A sacred awe should inspire us with the deepest humility, and lead us to pause in any arbitrary theory that might hinder an unbiassed reception of any lesson, from providential developements now rapidly transpiring. The sympathy of many believers has for some years been awakened respecting the natural Israel, and to minds of spiritual discernment, there seems something of true life, now ready to open dispensationally in their behalf. Not by the concentration of ecclesiastical power, or the wisdom of man, but by the dawning from on high, of the "SET TIME to favor Zion." At the begininng of the Gentile dispensation, when the divine ministration passed from the Jews to the Gentiles, the Apostle Paul said, "Have they stumbled that they should fall? God forbid; but rather, through their fall, salvation is come to the Gentiles. Now if the fall of them be the riches of the world, and the diminishing of them the riches of the Gentiles, how much more their fulness;" "for if the casting away of them be the reconciling of the world, what shall the receiving of them be, but life from the dead?" "For I would not, brethren, that ye should be ignorant of this mystery, lest ye should be wise in your own conceits, that blindness IN PART is happened to Israel UNTIL the fulness of the Gentiles come in." As the Lord Jesus, speaking in Luke of the time of his coming, saith of Israel; "They shall be led away captive into all nations, and Jerusalem shall be trodden down of the Gentiles UNTIL the times of the Gentiles be fulfilled." These Scriptures show, that the natural branches were only broken off for a determined season, in which time God would "visit the Gentiles, to take out of them a people for his name," to be grafted into the good olive tree; after which fulness, the natural branches will be grafted in again.

But to return to my experience: Since the time of my first expectation of the coming of the Lord, my soul has been gradually passing through deepening waters, of trial, sacrifice and refining, I can solemnly say, with one only desire and strife, to KNOW and obey the Lord. This course has cost me many sorrows, from grieving those I loved, and the loss of all things of this life. It is a serious thing, to yield our "spirit, soul, and body," "a living sacrifice to God," and to LIE DOWN on the altar of his will. In questions of daily and present duty, I have not dared to lean to my own understanding, nor the desire or wisdom of human teaching, but have chosen, at the risk of all consequences, which my natural sensitive, and cautious mind ever duly weighed, to prove the Lord in simple obedience to his *word*, his providence, and his Spirit. I BELIEVE, and desire humbly to practically receive, the living example and words of our blessed Lord, in his Sermon on the Mount, and the 12th of Luke, and elsewhere, as to the entire sacrifice, and consecration of our life; also, the possession of that divine ministry and teaching, which he enjoins in John xiv. 16, 17, 21, 26; also, John xvi. 7—15, respecting the reality of the person and mission of the Comforter; also, the testimony of the Apostle, Rom. viii. 4. 5, 9, 14, and Gal. v. 16, 18, 25; and I esteem it the blessed privilege of every believer so to walk as not to grieve "the Holy Spirit of God, by which we are sealed unto the day of redemption."

During these years of waiting, I saw the machinery of Gentile organizations becoming still more complicated and divided, and their wheels dragging heavily, as if the glory was departing, and sought the Lord much, with many tears, to know where the ark of his testimony was resting, and where was the moving and hiding of his power?

Such was the travail of my spirit, at one time, that I was confined to my bed for some days, when a passage of Scripture was strongly impressed upon my mind. 1 Chron. xi. 16, 17: "And David was then in the hold, and the Philistines' garrison was then at Bethlehem; and David longed, and said, Oh, that one would give me drink of the water of the well of Bethlehem, that is at the gate;" and the following lines were given me impromptu, in prayer, but I then understood little of their definite import:

In the Hold, long oppressed by Earth's wearisome strife,
My soul is athirst for the waters of Life—
And longs for the Well-spring at Beth-lehem's gate,
Where its fount gushes freely, this thirst to abate.

Oh! who will break THROUGH, in the strength of the Lord,
And at once overcome—by his Spirit and Word—
The uncircumcised Host, that opposeth His reign,
And bid the sweet waters of Life FLOW again?

Oh! who will "GO UP," and the Land now possess,
In the Name of the Highest his Sabbaths redress—
'Till the praise of that NAME in loud chorus shall rise,
From mountain and valley, from ocean and skies?

Oh! who shall BETWEEN the bright Cherubims PASS,
And restore the LOST garden of beauty at *last;*
Who shall give to its long desert bowers their bloom,
And say to the Saved, and the Ransomed RETURN?

For ONE we have waited, for ONE we have sought—
While lords and gods *many*, great wonders have wrought;
But NONE has brought forth—the SALVATION, the LOVE,
And we WAIT yet ANOTHER, to come from above.

His Name must be JESUS!—no other we know,
Who can BID the wide Stream of REDEMPTION to FLOW;
Who can BREAK through the Host, the Inheritance bless,
And RESTORE the LOST children of EDEN to REST.

For many months my mind was deeply exercised in spirit, and I was directed towards Jerusalem, though I had no outward reason for expectation, or spiritual profit for myself or others *there*. Long and agonizing was my inward struggle, against the thought of going. Outwardly, I had *every thing to lose*, and suffer; and inwardly nothing apparently to gain; but the conviction of my soul increased every hour, that God was calling me to go!—to forsake all, and venture wholly on him, without a reason why! But this was accompanied with a strong assurance, that my late prayer should be answered, and blessing would follow. At length I submitted, some months before the expected hour of leaving, and in silence began to make some little preparation. As I had no pecuniary means, and could ask no one for money, I rested on the certainty, that if the Lord did not provide so large a sum, in some extraordinary way of his own, I still should be spared the fearful sacrifice. Step by step, I slowly finished every preparatory arrangement of duty in my power. One week remained, and I had not received the money; but still felt a strange certainty that it would come. I had a few beloved friends in Christ, to whom with trembling I unburdened my heart, who, though they could not believe with me, had grace and love to bear with my bonds, but were astonished and grieved at my purpose; this increased my pain, and my pillow was nightly wet with tears. When four days remained, I received about half what my strictest need would demand, from a source from which I had not expected assistance. A few humble but praying, souls sympathised with my sore travail, and wrestled much with God for me. The last day came; and half an hour before I left, two dear friends, came in haste, and completed the sum, so long promised in spirit!! One said: "I could scarcely sleep last night, and can feel no rest till you are gone!!"——I was overcome, and compelled, by this peculiar manifestation, of the Divine will, for many casual hindrances might have prevented this sudden sacrifice of the pious donors, and I immediately set out, and they with the kindest sympathy rode with me to the river, as I must take the cars on the other side, expecting to find a sea-passage from New York. The inward struggle of my heart was great, as for the last time I looked into each silent room of my quiet home, which so long had been a Bethel to my soul, and where my prayers and tears had so often mingled. A little delay in conversation prevented our reaching the railway in time, and I was obliged to wait in Camden for another train. My faith was perplexed, at such a failure in the first step. I must here say, that I was entirely unadvised of the best Eastern route attainable, with my moderate means; having made much inquiry to little purpose; but the same evening I saw a paper advertising a vessel to sail immediately from Philadelphia to Marseilles. After prayer, I decided to wait, and inquire respecting it. It proved to be a common merchant vessel, owned and commanded by a Christian captain, from Maine, whose wife and daughter were accompanying him, and I engaged passage with him for about half the usual price!! from which circumstance, I felt satisfied with my late apparent hindrance.

JOURNAL FROM PHILADELPHIA

TO

JERUSALEM.

WRITTEN ON SHIPBOARD, MAY 16, 1849.

Upon Columbia's Ocean-cradled strand,
A watcher with prospective glass, I stand,
Far peering eastward, through the gathering gloom,
Where thickens darkest, Earth's approaching doom;
Nations and thrones, by heaving Earthquakes riven,
With pestilence, and war, and famine, driven.
And as the conflict deepens into night,
I wait till darkness shall give place to light,
With hope expectant, of a brighter day,
To drive these shades of sin and death away.
And now at length, as like a beacon star,
A radiance dawns, o' er Judah's HILLS afar—
The desolate and long-forsaken hearth,
That gave the oracles of wisdom birth,
The mount of Prophecy, the fount of Song,
"Vision of peace," the beautiful, the strong,
Zion ARISE! the measured time has come,
When thy dispersed, and torn, shall gather home,
For thy long night, of exile dire is past,
And "Gentile times," and rule, run out at last—
To greet thy Sons, and hail Earth's Jubilee,
I vènture forth, a pilgrim lone to be,
Across the broad waves' weary breast, to go,
And only rest where Shiloh's waters flow.

May 28, 1849.—These blank pages were presented to me, by a beloved friend, just before embarking, with my dear A——, on this voyage of many prayers and tears, in which, if health permit, I hope to pencil often by the way,

2

trusting that if we fail not in our errand, they may contain somewhat of interest, for such an one, on our return.

We have been now thirteen days on board, and our little bark has been so favored of the Lord with fair wind, that we are about half-way to Gibraltar, yet I have been so weak with sea-sickness, and my old difficulty, (dyspepsia,) together with the new and constant motion of the vessel, that this is the first moment I have been able to write. The change in our diet is so great, that nothing but the power and goodness of God can keep us. We have much for which to praise him, in our present condition. Captain P—— is a very kind, worthy man, and seeks to make us as comfortable as his circumstances will permit. We have more room than is usual in such vessels, and no other passengers, which gives us opportunity to think and pray.

May 29.—It is a bright and beautiful day. I am better in health, and have been able to walk on deck, and watch the far blue depth, stretching far and trackless around me. Oh, what a school and mystery is human life! I seem as in a dream! A few days since, I had a quiet home, and friends I loved; but now I am a weary stranger, a pilgrim on the sea. My heart still trembles, and my tears will flow at the strange sacrifice—unmurmuring! Beloved one, good night!

June 5.—To-day we are lying becalmed, in the neighborhood of the Azores, lat. 37. long. 29. So far there has been no incident worthy of relation. The last few days we have had light contrary winds, the weather cool and rainy, and motion sufficient to keep me from writing. I do not suffer severely, though still constantly affected with weakness and nausea of the stomach, and heat and oppression in the head. Our accommodations are as comfortable as we could expect; and but one serious occasion of uneasiness, which is, that our ship is old, and the pilot gave us a rub on one of the last sand-bars in the bay, since which the sailors have been obliged to pump nearly every hour! This gives us room for FAITH in GOD, as man cannot help us. Almost all our little comforts speak some cherished name, and bring up from our hearts a constant echo of love unfeigned. Oh, when shall the sweet moment of return, and redemption come, when the weary and the heavy-laden shall go home to an eternal rest? Nothing, but the consciousness that I am sincerely following the call of God, could give me hope in the dark and trying prospect before me. If I please HIM, I have gained every thing; if I have failed, I can but perish. I walk by FAITH, and not by sight, and know assuredly that I please not myself, and trust the issue with the Lord.

June 7.—We have had head winds for several days, and have been beating about nearly in the same neighborhood. This morning, the Captain's daughter went on deck, at the strange cry of "land ho!" and soon came down and reported to me, that we were near another shore, far away from our own beloved. After breakfast, I went up with her, and saw the Islands of Pico and Fayal nearly ahead. They seemed of a deep blue in the distance, and a beautiful wreath of white clouds girdled the high mountain peak of Pico. The view I here sketch, is imperfect on account of the rough head sea. This is the twenty-third day since we came on board, and although the time seems long, we have great reason to praise the Lord for his sustaining and preserving love.

In the afternoon we ran in near to the Islands, and passed four in number. Their appearance is different from any thing I have before seen, the centre of each is the highest, from which the surface slopes, with more or less inequality and undulations to the shore. I saw no forest trees; but the soil is all carefully cultivated, garden-like, with the spade, and laid out in small squares, or beds, with vegetables, potatoes, grain, and several varieties of fruit and vines. These tiny patches, and their varying hues of color, seem, in the distance, like one beautiful mosaic extending over mount and vale. The Island of Graciosa (the Spanish of Gracious) I think is the most beautiful of the group; in gentle undulations, orange-groves, vines, etc., like one entire garden, spotted with small, white cottages. At the south end, there is a considerable town; I saw two steeples, and some fine buildings. Here, I am told, they have no frost, and no venomous reptiles, and the inhabitants enjoy a summer's sky, far away from the great world's bustle. Its loveliness was enhanced by the long ocean-waste, over which we have just passed, and I sighed for the New Earth—Paradise. They are Portuguese, and rent the soil of feudal owners, and are under the Roman Catholic religion.

June 17.—Yesterday we made the Cape of St. Vincent, the southern extremity of Portugal; and to-day we have just hailed the dim outlines of the neighborhood of Gibraltar, and the far African coast. My heart weeps for thy wrongs, Oh, Africa! the sunny home, our Father once gave to his dark-browed children, who now, by their brethren's hand, are homeless and bound!

We are sailing opposite Cape Trafalgar, and as I look at the history of the past, the waters beneath us seem dyed in blood, and I shudder at the thought of the scenes of piracy and war, (legalized murder,) that have crimsoned their tide.

In this vicinity, my own father, long since, was seized with his vessel, and carried lawlessly into Algiers, and condemned to be a prisoner for life! But God rescued him from the Algerine, and restored him to his young wife's prayers and tears. I can say little that is interesting concerning our voyage, as I have been much indisposed; yet the tender mercy of the Lord has been constantly with me. There has been no storm, but light winds and cool nights. My sensations are new and strange! Another world opens to my sight; before, I have only seen it by faith, but now, my senses demonstrate its reality. So shall we soon prove the existence of the unseen, and spiritual world, spoken of by many witnesses, in the Scriptures. Several fishing boats are near, full of robust, dark looking forms they cheered us kindly, and strove to throw some of their fish on to our deck, showing that they are human, and belong to the same great brotherhood of man. The sand, rocks, and irregular hills, bear the same Maker's impress as those in our own dear land. The sky is just as blue and bright, and the white clouds, in beauty float above, the very same, as in the long June days they rest over the green banks of the Schuylkill and Delaware. It is our first warm day, and a quiet breeze, with the ceaseless current running from the Atlantic to the Mediterranean, is floating us rapidly toward the Straits. This kindly welcome, from these stranger fishermen, is a sweet token that our Father in heaven can turn all foreign hearts from harm, towards his defenceless pilgrims. Beloved friend, good night!

June 18.—The wind fell as we came near the Straits, and I made a sketch at sunset, of the lighthouse on point Tarifa, the southern extremity of Spain, 15 miles outside the rock of Gibraltar; and on the opposite shore, of the rock of Abyla, the northern point of Africa. This latter, with the rock of Gibraltar, were styled by the ancients the Pillars of Hercules, which mark a most interesting point between two continents, an ocean 3000 miles wide behind, and a sea 2500 miles before us, on a track more beaten than any on the deep seas.

June 19.—In the night a head wind arose, and we beat our way, until at sunrise we came near the celebrated rock of Gibraltar. The sea is very rough, but I have succeeded in getting a hasty outline, of its first appearance, as we approached it, nearly opposite the light-house. I have been suffering much, for a few days past with dyspepsia, and begin to long for the shore.

June 21.—We are becalmed, and only fifty miles from the Straits! The weather is very fine, but the delay is wearisome. I have been looking, for the first time (since they were given me at leaving home,) at two daguerreotypes, all I have with me, and what a thrill of tenderness sweeps over my heart as I look at these beloved shadows—kind helpers of my better life, whose Christian sympathy is with me still, "without the camp." The LORD REMEMBER and reward your love!

My sensations are peculiar and mixed, as I look round on this new hemisphere! The air is bland; the sky exceeding blue, and the light and shadowy clouds, like snowy wreaths of flowers; the distant hills, on the Spanish coast, in dim but picturesque outline, while the calm waters of the blue Mediterranean glisten in the sunlight around me. I seem lost in undefined reverie! Is it myself? and am I approaching the classic shores of my early imaginings? when all would have been Elysian! But how unlike my former self! How changed my hopes and my ambition! I still LOVE the pure and the beautiful; but my heart seeketh, and RESTETH alone, in that which is fadeless and true. I still love, and love with more devotion, *all* that our Father in heaven hath made; ALL, the least that are lovely, in form or spirit, with sympathetic COMPLACENCE—according to their approximation to the DIVINE; and ALL things, animate and intelligent, that are unlovely through estrangement from God, I love with earnest benevolence. From the feverish thirst, the impulsive inspirations of my own restless spirit, I have turned, and seek to follow the light that shineth within my heart from Heaven. So SURE as there is a genius, and a gift of mind, in man, while he is in nature and unsanctified, so SURE, there IS a higher, more spiritual, and true intelligence, and power, received from the Author of LIFE and wisdom, by those who are WEARY, and fully turn from the broken cisterns of a self-life, and seek only the TRUE, and the ETERNAL—the LOVE, that cannot die.

June 22.—The weather is warm and fine; the sea calm, with only an occasional gentle breeze. It is thirty-eight days since we sailed, and they seem longer than they do on shore. We are just now drifting near the Spanish coast, which appears, from this distance, like one range of barren mountains, rocky and sterile, with some eminences of considerable height, covered with snow. After the activity and excitement of the last few years, how strange is this quietude—this almost vacuum of existence! and leisure for thoughtful reminiscence, which is only broken by the often recurring necessities of ship circumstances. Those around me are all occupied with any thing but my heart's treasure, and its language and burden unknown by them. Oh, how I long to finish the work that has been given me to do, and to see the beloved of my soul, even Jesus, in his coming glory!

June 28.—We are still hindered by alternate calms and contary winds, along the Spanish coast. One mountain rock appears so beautiful, encircled mid-way with a wreath of white mist, that I here send a poor sketch; the declivity on one side is thickly dotted with olive trees, and our chart calls it "Olivio." Several picturesque boats are skimming along near its base, with fanciful, butterfly looking sails.

July 1. We are slowly moving forward on the calm summer sea, opposite Barcelona, some 200 miles from Marseilles, our FIRST port. Patience and hope are strangely blended, and I do not envy the poor sailor his home upon the waters.

July 3.—As we approached the far-famed "Gulf De Lion," we met a heavy sea, which was soon followed by a severe gale of wind. Our poor vessel rolled and pitched fearfully, and the waves roared truly lion-like. To-day it is subsiding; we are in sight of France, some thirty miles from our expected port. Truly great has been the preserving mercy of our God, in thus far bringing us safely on our pilgrimage.

July 6.—On the 4th inst. we arrived in Marseilles. The harbor is very peculiar; a narrow inlet runs up from the sea a few miles; it is fenced on each side by high, naked rocks; becomes very narrow, and opens into a deep oblong basin, which receives the shipping, and the city is thickly built around it, with citadels and towers crowning the natural rock defence at the entrance.

But there are few trees; my weary eyes have in vain looked for *forest* foliage, upon the distant heights of the Azores, Portugal, Gibraltar, Spain and France, along the coast. Oh! give me back the green hills and waving forest trees again!

The city is very ancient, and was in existence before our Saviour's time. Oh! how many footsteps, joyous and sad, have come and gone! The houses look very uninviting to my unaccustomed eye, more like prisons than cheerful homes; and most unlike the clean painted dwellings of Philadelphia. The strange plaintive tone of the last syllable of this foreign tongue, the various dress, manners, colors, and features, all confuse and oppress the poor pilgrims; and, as we pass the narrow, crowded streets, we see Turks, Greeks, Moors, and Italians, all pressing on, in the bewildering strife of natural existence. My spirit looks to catch one eye, that beams with the meek love of God. Where shall I find one? I may not, but our heavenly Father knoweth every Noah, and every Lot, whose righteous souls may be vexed at the surrounding iniquity here. But it is late, BELOVED friend; good night, good night!

July 8.—We have two rooms, at four and a half francs per day, in a large lodging house, which is occupied by different families, who rent furnished apartments at a stated price, without board. They have their meals brought from a restauraut, or they can order any thing from the common kitchen, at a separate charge. The expense of living seems to be about the same as at home. We have experienced serious difficulty on account of not understanding the French language, in obtaining lodgings, and suitable food, and the necessary information respecting the best route eastward, as very few persons speak English, and the citizens know as little about Jerusalem, as they do in the United States. We have inquired of our Consul, but he cannot direct us. A missionary from the Church of England has called to see us; he says, that he has a congregation of about twenty hearers! that although there are many English residents, merchants, etc., there are few that have any interest in religion! He could tell us nothing of the way to Palestine.

In this extremity we were much perplexed, and set apart most of the time yesterday, to entreat the Lord for help, and guidance. It proved to be a season of peculiar blessing; we were much strengthened, and urged in spirit, to hasten away from this land, whose soil is stained with the blood of many martyrs of Jesus! It was also sensibly presented to our minds, while in prayer, that there is at least one poor Israelite in Jerusalem, who will receive us, and is fainting for help! Soon after, a young gentleman, whom we had not seen before, knocked at our door, and in broken English, apologized for his visit. He said that he had heard of our case, and came to offer us any assistance in his power. Ever since, he has been exerting himself in our behalf, and though the weather is extremely hot, he has been on board of several steamers, out in the harbor, searched the papers, and visited offices, and agents, to secure for us the best and cheapest route. He has just returned from an excursion to Constantinople, and has given us much late and useful intelligence. He has rooms in the same building, and calls every hour or two, to speak for any thing we wish. He is intelligent, and refined in his manners, and treats us with the kindest attention. While we feel the most sincere gratitude and esteem for him, we KNOW that it is THE LORD, that has sent him to our relief, and would acknowledge his persevering love, in this timely aid.

July 10. This afternoon we expect to leave Marseilles by the English line of steamers from this place to Alexandria. Pierre Hugenot, our kind friend, has been truly a helper, in our necessary arrangements; may the blessing of the stranger's God rest upon him! We have just parted with our American friends, on board the vessel on which we came; they have been very kind, and we must ever esteem Capt. P——, his lady and daughter, with Christian regard. As our heaviest trunk was taken over the side of the vessel, it fell into the water, and sank, as we supposed to rise no more, but, to the surprise of the sailors, it came up again, and they secured it. For this we would thank the Lord, as we could have scarcely proceeded without the plain necessary clothing which it contained.

July 12.—On board the British mail steamer for Malta. We have very few passengers, on account of it being the hot season. One English officer of the army, and lady, and some others, *en route* for India. The accommodations in the first cabin are good; the fare is £9; but we are in the second cabin, and the fare is £5; it is situated directly under the first, and we have no air, excepting through a grating in its floor above us! The heat is very oppressive, and I am writing on the forward deck. The poor sailors are bustling around me, and we cannot have the privilege of an awning, when the sails are set. Imagination already begins to add to the present the opening vista before us, the arid sands, and scorching sun of Egypt! but my only trust and hope is in the Lord, that he will strengthen me to endure all things which he hath appointed, and help me to overcome, and return to the precious and beloved ones, from whom we are now so far separated.

July 13.—At Malta, where the Apostle of the Gentiles was shipwrecked. We have changed steamers, and are now on board of another of the same line, to leave immediately for Alexandria, Egypt. The fare is £12, 10 shillings in the first, and £7, 5 shillings in the second cabin. The island appears from the sea like a barren pile of rock; the high clay-looking walls of the houses are built irregularly, one above another, around a small inlet harbor. The heat is excessive, and my heart almost melts at the bustle, and noise of the English war-ships anchored near, and the strange and heartless bearing of the natives and port-officers. Oh, when I think of the far away beloved, among the sweet groves and cool streams of our own dear land, my spirit would fain whisper to them, to value more, with grateful love to God, their Eden heritage. I am informed that there is considerable cultivation here upon soil that has been brought in vessels from neighboring islands, and that this soil must be occasionally renewed.

July 14.—The power of the sun increases, and scarcely a breath of wind ruffles the glassy surface of the sea, as our good steamer is bearing away, southeast by east, towards the coast of Africa. The strict order and parade of a war-vessel is preserved on the steamers of this line: but THIS commander (of the Medina) has kindly given us the liberty of the quarter-deck, under its thick awning, and allowed me a berth in the first cabin, where the port-holes are open, which is a great mercy from the Lord in my present weak state. I dare not anticipate what may await me in Egypt, in the uncertainty of further means of progress eastward, and the hazard of expensive suffering detention in Alexandria. While I deeply realize the cost of the sacrifice of all behind me, the pain of the present, and the darkness and peril of the future, with a solemn purpose of soul, I would count them all as nothing, so I may please the Lord, and accomplish his will.

July 20.—Arrived at Alexandria the 17th instant. The coast is sandy and low; there are many wind-mills in motion near the entrance of the harbor; on the west side, just within, stands the palace of the Pasha; high stone buildings, with windows only in the upper stories, and others rough-looking and very inferior, extend with little order back from the sea. It is the sickly season, and none of the steamer's crew were permitted to land. We were soon surrounded with their queer-looking, heavy boats; Turkish officers, agents, natives, etc., came on board, and all haste was made to despatch the mail and passengers on shore; a few connected with the business of the steamer spoke English. Among these was a resident, who conducted us to the house of the American Consul. He was surprised that we should come in the most unfavorable and sickly season, when any delay in Egypt would be perilous, and informed us that the English steamer to Jaffa, in which we expected to go, carried only the mail, and on account of the quarantine could take no passengers, which rendered our position most perplexing, and was a severe trial of my faith. He called his Arab Janisary and interpreter, and directed him to assist us in the best possible arrangement. He is tall, fine-looking, and intelligent, and has proved to be very kind and energetic in serving us. There are two expensive hotels kept here, in English style; but he procured us comfortable lodgings, at two dollars per day, in an Italian house.—From the effect of the heat, the excitement and fatigue of landing and walking in the sun, I was immediately attacked with symptoms of dysentery, and was confined to my bed while we remained on shore. After we were settled, our new friend, Ali Hamet, set about obtaining a passage for us in a sailing vessel. He returned several times without success, expressing much concern for us. I found that there was no regular communication with Jaffa, and that there was no prospect of a vessel leaving for that place, for a month. A French steamer, on her way to Beyroot, stops here regularly, but left a few days before we arrived.—Yesterday the harbor-master gave him notice, that a small brig was about leaving for Beyroot; but that it was filled with rice, and had no cabin or awning, or accommodations for board! Beyroot is over a hundred miles beyond Jaffa, and it will cause us great expense and detention to go there; but it has frequent communication with Jaffa, and is our only resource. Ali sought the Turkish captain, and directed him to make us a tent over his long boat, well lashed in the middle of the vessel, agreed for a moderate fare, and then ran all over the city to purchase the necessary stores and furniture for the voyage, which collection was most novel to me. This is a new way of traveling, but I will hope all things, and venture forward. He then came for us, took charge of the baggage through the custom-house, (having two Arabs to carry it before him,) and brought donkeys for us, not much above the size of a large dog. Numbers of half-covered men and boys crowded around and followed us, each striving to lead the donkeys or carry some bag or umbrella for a reward. The scene was like a strange caricature; Ali brandishing his plated staff (an insignia of his office,) with one hand, and holding a string of crying chickens in the other, going before to turn aside the droves of laden camels, mules, and donkeys that were pressing upon us in the mingled crowd. The custom officers honored him by passing our trunks unopened for a small fee, and we took a boat, and reached the brig near the mouth of the harbor. I can scarcely describe my sensations, as we approached; it is a small vessel with no bulwarks, so heavily laden, as to leave but a few feet above the water, and literally covered with human beings, seated on rough rolls of matting, which were laid closely over the cargo of rice. A strange chattering and hallooing commenced between Ali and the crew; the captain was on shore, and the long boat was not prepared.—At length Ali succeeded in clearing away a spot in the centre, where we and our baggage were deposited in the midst of the astonished gaze of our disturbed neighbors. All were talking, but we could understand nothing, and the only one with whom we could communicate must now leave us. We sat several hours holding our umbrellas, in suffering suspense, until the Captain, (a dark, turbaned man, in a loose dress,) came with the boat from the shore. Ali also returned; it was hoisted in, mats spread, and a low tent contrived over us; we cannot stand upright, but sit on the floor like our neighbors. Our trunks are in one end, a large Egyptian basket with provisions, and cooking and table apparatus in the other, and we have each a quilt, carpet-bag and cloak, which must serve for beds, pillows, and sofa.

July 21.—We are still waiting for wind, and seeking to accommodate ourselves to our new circumstances. The great yearly fast of the Moslems has commenced; and they call it Ram-a-*dan*. There are a number of the Pasha's great war-ships near us; they are dressed in all the various colored flags of the Ottoman tribes; I have just counted above seventy that are different on one ship. The war-steamers, ships, and forts have been playing a fearful roundelay of *heavy* guns, covering the water round us with thick smoke. The appearance of the passengers, men, women, and children, with a great variety of complexion, feature, and costume, is very novel and picturesque.—Among them are Greeks, Moors, Egyptians and Arabs; the skin of the Africans is more fine, glossy, and jet than any I have seen at home. All wear large turbans—a few white, but mostly of the highest colors, and have generally long beards. Their coarsest garments are decked with borders of gay contrast colors; they have generally a close vest, and a full short skirt, confined below the knees, like trousers. They also wear girdles of broad belting, or gay cotton stuff, bound heavily round the waist, and then a loose garment, or mantle, thrown across the shoulders. There is a different arrangement in the skirt with the women, and a loose thin covering, the size of a large shawl, variously attached to the head, hanging carelessly over the shoulders; below this, a piece of thin black cotton stuff is closely bound across the face, just below the eyes, covering the nose and mouth, which must occasion great suffering in this extreme heat. Some poor creatures, otherwise half covered, are scrupulous to obey this absurd law of human fashion! During Ram-a-*dan* they fast, and only eat one meal after sunset. We have but one cook to serve us all, and he is very busy towards evening preparing this meal. Some melons, squashes, beans, lentils, and rice, are boiled together, which composes a thick soup; this is poured out in large wooden bowls; these are set down on a mat, and pieces of dark-looking, hard bread laid round, according to the number to eat from each. In this way each family are served, and master and wife, and children and *slaves*, all sit round together; then there is silence, some are counting beads, and most lips are moving in seeming prayer, then all put in their fingers alternately, and eat together in silence. After this they began most piteous chanting, not in concert, but every one has his own song, sometimes the sounds break out in bold deep utterance, and then die away in the most unearthly wail, chattering and changing continually, without tune or measure. I sit listening, and imagine it is sincere devotional aspiration, and so unite and enjoy it well. They all speak Arabic, and the sound seems incoherent and rude. Ali came in a boat just now to take leave of us, and brought a kind note from the Consul.* We have become much interested in this child of Ishmael; his attention and kindness has been peculiar, and he has improved every opportunity of conversation with us; he confesses faith in God, and a habit of prayer, and a hope of one day living in Jerusalem! At parting he seemed much affected, and was unwilling to receive the usual present. Our meeting with such a kind and efficient helper in this moment of desperate need, we esteem as a great favor from the Lord. But the light is fading in my little tent; and we have no lamps, so I must close. Dear friend, good night!

* For whose sympathy and assistance we are more indebted than to any other, in all our tedious journey.

July 22.—We are out at sea, and our heavy craft is creening along, before a gentle breeze, towards the coast of Palestine. The sea-air has revived my drooping strength, and we have made acquaintance with a poor Jew, by the name of Solomon Lubhar, who is returning from Algiers to his family in Jerusalem. I remember a few words of French and Italian, with which he is a little acquainted, and he has five or six of English, so that I have commenced a list of Arabic words by his teaching. He seems to fill Ali's place, and kindly anticipates our wants; in the heat of the day he borrows mats, and covers our thin tent, and is our waiter and agent with the Arab cook. This is a great favor, as we cannot make any one else understand us. We have a chicken boiled with rice for dinner, and a pot of Mocha coffee morning and evening, which, with bread, raisins, and oil, constitute our living.—We have become somewhat intimate with our neighbors, who seem kind, and seek to oblige and do us good, in many little ways. There is scarcely an article on ship-board, or among their stores or baggage, but they have brought and repeated its name, in Arabic, for me to learn. Several are afflicted with sore eyes; and having a suitable ointment with me, it gave me an opportunity of some return; this they have highly appreciated, and a number have been relieved.

July 25.—This is the seventh day that we have been on this Turkish bark, and we make slow progress; we have had calms and light winds most of the way. At one time, a contrary wind arose, and all hands were called to trim the sails. The captain or mate, is always at the helm, and despite of their efforts, the brig turned round and round, and was heading for Egypt most of the time until it abated!! A winter voyage would be perilous with such navigators. About noon to-day, there was a general outcry, and I saw the young leaping and clapping their hands, and several faces peeped under our canvass, saying, Terra! Terra! I looked out, and behold!—the long-sought PROMISED land appeared, like a beautiful shadowy line in the distance.* It is indeed the same that I have so often traced on the sacred page, from my infant years, until now, my pilgrim vision greets its dear reality. It is the coast between Joppa and Beyroot, and is included in the promise to Abraham.

July 27.—We are still upon the sea, which is smooth as glass, with an occasional zephyr breeze. We are only half a day's sail from Beyroot, near the shore; sailing on the Mediterranean in summer, is tedious and uncertain, on account of such light winds. The appearance of the land is very beautiful, unlike any I have seen by the way, not wild and barren, but has gentle hills and vales, and mountains rising in the distance. It is not rock, but arable soil, shaded and spotted with green trees and vines. It is seventy-three days since we embarked at Philadelphia, and we are still floating wearily, and are now detained, day after day, in sight of the long-sought shore. I sometimes fear it is a rebuke for my weak and trembling faith, for many before me, have not been "able to enter in because of their unbelief!" When I look back across the sea, as the sun sinks, in the far, far West, I recall the beloved ones of my soul, and think what a surprise would seize them, if they could have one glance at the pilgrims, surrounded by their dark chattering companions; but it is sweet to know, that One there is who ever sees, and watches for our good. *Addio!*

Aug. 17.—Oh! my dear friend, a long time has elapsed, since I have been able to write, and I have suffered many things, of which I will briefly speak. The next morning after my last date, (July 28th,) before light, I heard an unusual stir among the sailors, and in a few moments they began to tear away the awning over us, and to make signs of lifting out the boat. We were unable to understand their design, or remonstrate, and were ejected suddenly, having little time to secure loose articles of

* Here I took a sketch, as the view was very beautiful, with gentle hills rising from the sea, shaded with foliage. I regret that these sketches by the way must be omitted.

baggage. When it was day, we saw the city of Beyroot some miles distant; there was no wind, and the sailors were rowing in the boat ahead of the vessel, towing us slowly into the harbor. As we drew near, we lost the sea air, and the power of the sun was such that I nearly fainted, we could have no meals, and the Nile water had become poor and warm. About noon they cast anchor, but were still distant from the laud. We were obliged then to wait several hours until the captain raised a yellow flag, and went ashore, to get an officer from the Quarantine, to come on board, and conduct us to its safe keeping.

At length a large boat came for us, we and our baggage were first placed in its centre, and I began to hope, that I should now be delivered from the fear, and near contact of the vermin, with which our poor neighbors were infested. This thought was soon dissipated, as they began to heap in all their bedding and baggage, and then piled the owners, in a promiscuous crowd around us! A young Greek, whose eyes had been relieved by the ointment, seemed to think that he had a favorable opportunity of expressing his gratitude, and with difficulty pressed his way, and seated himself close to my side. In vain I made signs of remonstrance, pointing to the creeping plague on his garments, he still retained his position, until we landed. There was a gentle surf beating into a little cove before us, and Solomon, to prevent the shock against the boat, sprang out suddenly, and took me in his arms, and set me on the shore. This was unexpected, and affected me much at the time, as I esteem him a devout son of Abraham, who thus welcomed me to his Father-land.

The Quarantine is composed of rows of low apartments, with a door and a window opening to the sea, and built on a point of rocks, on the north side of the harbor and city, about a mile distant, near the foot of a range of Mount Lebanon, that here runs down to the sea. Here we were met by several Turkish officers, and waited some time on the beach, till an assortment and disposal of the baggage and passengers could be made. The superintendent spoke a little English, and two rooms were assigned to us; and Solomon, at my request, was permitted access to them, and we soon found that our case would have been desperate without him. The walls and floors were roughly plastered, and entirely empty, without an article of furniture. A small colored man was appointed guardian over us, to keep us from escaping, to lock us in every night, and bring our water, etc. We had his board and salary to pay, beside a heavy government tax for the rooms and other officials, who supply travelers with provisions, and furniture, at an advanced price of their own. Sick and fasting, I sat down upon my trunk, and Solomon, ran and bought of them two large mats. These were laid down, and my quilt and cloak spread upon one; and this was my bed several days; (after which I became so ill that he obtained a mattress of the Superintendent, and during our twelve days imprisonment I was unable to sit up an hour, having a severe attack of dysentery.) Here we found the importance of the supply of provisions, and the cooking utensils, which we had brought from Egypt. Solomon bought charcoal, and in a corner of the room, where there was an aperture to let out the smoke, he kindled a fire, boiled some rice, and made us coffee. We then returned most solemn thanks to God, for his preserving mercy, in bringing us thus far on our way, and permitting us to reach the land of the Bible, and committed ourselves anew to his holy keeping.

Our fellow passengers were all confined in rooms near us, and hearing that I was ill, were often at my door inquiring, and some that were taken with fever, they would bring in to seek my advice, (two severe cases, by the blessing of God, on some simple remedies, applied by Solomon's aid, were recovered,) supposing from the effect of the ointment that I had farther skill. One day, when my symptoms were such, that I had little hope of life, a Turk, who was in dress and manners superior to the rest, came bowing in, to the side of my mat, and unwrapped his ankle and leg, which was full of ulcers, and looked piteously in my face, saying to Solomon, that he had not slept for many nights; I thought it was probably my last opportunity of doing any thing for Jesus' sake, and directed Solomon to sponge it with warm water, and then sat up in bed, and was strengthened to spread some ten or twelve plasters, and apply to the sores. He then unbound his turban, which was an embroidered mull-scarf, and tore a square from one end, with which he carefully wrapped the whole, and retired. Next day he came expressing great joy, having slept well all night. He continued to improve until we left, and manifested much regard for us. Solomon was very kind and attentive, seemed concerned, and often prayed for me, standing upright with his face to the east, and bowing his head to the ground. As I lay on my low and suffering bed, I reflected upon the step of faith that had led me there; and was astonished at the sustaining love of God, which lifted my soul above despair. Musquitoes were numerous, and had a poisonous effect; for my face and hands were covered with dark, red spots, as if I had just recovered from the small-pox. Fleas were also very troublesome, and large; and lizards crept up and down, familiarly upon the walls. On arriving, I wrote a note to our Consul, requesting his assistance, in securing us a passage to Jaffa, as soon as our Quarantine should end. I received in answer, that the English steamer that leaves Beyroot, once a month, with passengers for Jaffa, would leave before our time was out, and that we should be obliged to wait another month! This prospect was very distressing, as dysentery and fever, were raging in the city, and an English physician assures me that there is more fatality than during the Cholera last year, or in fourteen years previous! also, there is but one comfortable hotel, and its charges are beyond our means! To increase my distress, every specimen of bread, which I could obtain in Beyroot, was *so sour*, that the Superintendent said "it taste Lee-mon;" meaning like lemons, which, in my diseased state, it was impossible to eat. I had still a few crackers, which I had brought from Egypt, but the heat was such that they had become full of worms; these I partly separated and soaked, which, with a little sweet oil and rice, composed my diet.

At length our prison was unlocked, and two Arabs, with a boat from the Consul, came for us, with a note that they would put us on board of an Arab Felluka going to Jaffa. I had become greatly emaciated and so weak, that with difficulty I reached the boat. After rowing a mile in the sun, we reached a small open craft, without a deck or awning!! Two or three dark, wild-looking men, with no dress, but a short apron around their waist, pulled us in, and cleared away a spot among the ballast, to spread my mat! I was exhausted with pain and fatigue, and lay down with my umbrella over my face. Solomon brought some water, and hung up some pieces of old matting over me! I then strove to compose my mind to die, and lifted my heart to God, entreating that for Jesus' sake, he would accept the offering of my life. I had only about a pint of those poor crackers left, the prospect of the burning sun, an indefinite time at sea, and greater difficulties at Jaffa! But language can scarcely speak my suffering position! Just before we left the Quarantine, as from my bed, I was looking out of the door westward upon the sea, I saw a fine ship entering the harbor, with a large flag flying in the wind, and remarked that if it were a possibility, I should think it was the American flag, but repressed the idea, and thought no more of it. This, however, proved to be the case, and was the signal messenger, which was used of the Lord, to save me! But to return to the Arab boat; towards evening, Solomon took some charcoal to their caboose, to make us some coffee; but they refused him the privilege! As it grew dark, we were reflecting upon our state, and beseeching the mercy of the Lord, when we heard an English voice, calling our names. This seemed more like illusion, than reality, until we saw a boat alongside, and the Captain of the American ship just mentioned! He told us afterward, that he had heard of us incidentally, at the Consul's that afternoon, and had sought for us in vain on his return to his ship. That, after tea, his mind was so much exercised about us, that he entered his boat again, though so near dark, to venture in strange waters among the Arab fleet of boats that surrounded us, with no other clue but our name! After inquiring into our situation, he kindly invited us to come on board of his vessel in the morning. He then left, and in a short time his boat returned, with a liberal supply of the finest ship bread, and several varieties of crackers, cakes, etc! This unexpected providence—in this destitute region, in our state of *suffering* and *danger*, in the *night*, on the *sea*, among *Arabs*, can scarcely be truly appreciated, by others, in its sudden effect upon our hearts. Our moaning prayer was turned into thanksgiving and joy, as if an angel had been sent down from heaven to our relief! We received it as the direct interposition of our heavenly Father, who hears the raven's cry and careth for the sparrow's fall.

Next morning, before the sun was up, we made signs to the Arabs to carry us on board of the strange ship; but they could not understand, until Solomon held up three fingers, to shew its three masts, as there was none like it in the harbor. Capt. H——n received us kindly, and advised us to abandon our Arab boat, and wait on board of his ship, until the second of next month, when the steamer will leave for Jaffa! This generous offer we gladly accepted, and sent for our baggage. Solomon came back with the boat, to bid us farewell. He wept and made the most affecting signs of grief, that he could not go with us to Jerusalem! and was scarcely reconciled with our promise to seek him there. This strange and sudden deliverance seems too bright to be reality, and we feel as if we were in a pleasant dream! The beautiful barque of Captain H——n is in perfect order, and cleanliness, comfort, and good taste, are unusually combined. His Lady, and their only child, a lovely little girl of three years, are with him; also Mr. S——h, the supercargo. The Consul says, this is the first American merchant vessel that has ever visited Beyroot! and they have had the surprizing rapid passage of thirty-seven days from New York! The saloon, and state rooms are large, and well furnished, and the table is supplied with the best New York stores, and the daily addition of fresh meat, fowls, eggs, milk, figs, grapes, peaches, and plumbs, from the shore. But this minute narration will weary you, and I hope that I shall not again be so long hindered from writing.

Aug. 18.—When I first came on board, I was so weak and ill I could sit up but a little; but now I am rapidly regaining strength, and enjoy an excellent appetite. It is "the time of the first ripe grapes," which are brought to us from Lebanon. I have ventured to eat freely of them, and they have greatly refreshed me. We are anchored so far from the shore, that we have the sea-breeze, and do not suffer from the heat, which is very oppressive in the city. When I reflect, that if this vessel had been an ordinary time on her way, I must have perished, I am filled with grateful surprise, at the wonderful love of God to his unworthy child.

Aug. 20.—Soon after we came on board, the Captain, and his lady, and daughter, and Mr. S——h, went about fifteen miles up the mountains of Lebanon, to see the American missionaries, who reside there in summer, at the village of Arbay. On the third day of their visit, the child was taken with dysentery, and died after five day's illness. A poor sailor, belonging to the vessel also died, and was buried on the same day. Their graves are near that of Lieutenant Dale, who accompanied the United States' Exploring Expedition to the Dead Sea, and died here last year, on his return. Capt. H——n was also taken ill, and could not attend the burial, and is still unable to return to the ship. Mr. S——h, and the first mate, and the steward, have the same symptoms; and it is a solemn time on board. We truly sympathize with the afflicted parents, for the child was one of unusual beauty and promise.

Aug. 21.—Here we are still floating on the sea, and waiting for entrance into the promised land; and it is yet twelve days before the steamer leaves. Two missionaries spent the night on board, having returned with Captain H——n, who has recovered from his recent attack. They appear like pious, practical men, and in conversation they complained of a general declension in living faith, as the greatest hindrance to their work, in themselves and others.

Towards evening, as the power of the sun decreases, I sit upon the upper deck, and look away from the city over the sea, where the sun sets in the blue waters. How mingled and tender are my emotions, as I stand on this extreme eastern verge of the Mediterranean, and look westward its entire length through the Straits of Gibraltar, and onward still, across the Atlantic's billowy waste, until at length my spirit's eye rests on the green shore of our own dear land; and then each well remembered name and place, in thrilling life, comes to my heart, embracing all in silent prayer! Father! preserve, *preserve* spotless, unblamable, those names, until HE COME, our long-expected, and the weary shall go home.

As the sun declines, it enlarges, and becomes of the brightest scarlet hue, and the thin veil-like clouds and sky deepen from light orange, at the zenith, to the darkest richest copper near the sea. On the other side of the ship I see Beyroot, with its light-colored stone-houses, interspersed with vines and mulberry trees, rising, terrace-like, from the beach, with here and there a mosque's tall minaret—a lofty palm—a ruined citadel. Then northward, a range of Lebanon, towering above the lower clouds, rises abruptly from the sea, and stretches inland, forming a sublime background for the city. Its surface is very rocky and irregular, with hills rising one above another, divided by deep ravines. The general appearance, from this distance, looks naked and ash-like, with no forest foliage; but in places the soil is cultivated in terraces, and I see villages of little huts, surrounded by low mulberry, fig and olive trees, and vines. The missionaries say, that wherever there is a spring there is a village, from which the natives drink and water their flocks. The best fruit and vegetables are brought from these heights, on donkeys, to the city. But I am digressing too long from my heart's burden—a pilgrim by faith to Jerusalem—hindered by the way; but I hope in God, and *trust* him still, that he will surely bring me through. My heart runs out in love which I cannot speak, to the dear believing ones at home, and all their loveliness in grace seems increased an hundred-fold by the weary time and distance, as here I muse and pray.

Aug. 29.—We have been on shore several times, towards evening; but the heat is very oppressive, and the air is impure in the city, and I returned to the vessel with increased gratitude unto the Lord for providing us such a breeze-rocked cradle on the sea. At the Italian Hotel we met with Sir Moses Montefiori, on his return from Jerusalem, who, with his lady, treated us with much kindness, and gave us information and advice about the route, and the state of things there. He represented the Jews as in a state of great wretchedness and poverty, and remarked that if there are any true hearts in Israel that deserve sympathy and aid, it is surely those who cling, in such destitution and devotion, to the dust of their fathers in Jerusalem. He said that this is the third visit to them, and that he intends, if Providence permit to see them again next summer. He seemed much pleased with what he termed the enthusiasm of Major Noah, of New York, in his late address, and regretted that there was so little reality in the advance of the Jews in Jerusalem, and that great liberality is needful among *all* people for the general good. He has a very noble form and stature, and kind and intelligent features, and we returned much pleased with the bland and social manners of this Jewish nobleman.

How many believers in Jesus and the Holy Scriptures spend their time and money, with danger and fatigue, to visit the classic remains of pagan philosophy, of *deified* men and heroes, whose elevation mostly consists in the greatest number of men conquered! enslaved! butchered! But how *few* who humbly seek to worship God, in "the place of the name of the Lord of Hosts," and offer the sacrifice of praise and thanksgiving for a Saviour's love at Bethlehem, at Nazareth and Calvary,—to honor a greater than Cæsar, Socrates, or Cicero—one "who spake as never man spake!" A visit and eulogy to the sculptured chroniclers of these is highly esteemed, while a pilgrimage to the shades of Gethsemane is often regarded by a Christian world as enthusiasm and *fanaticism!* I have learned something of this prejudice from remarks of various travellers and dignitaries by the way, respecting former tourists to Palestine, notwithstanding which, I can testify to a kind and constant Providence, who has given us favor with all men. We have not experienced one harsh word, or unkind act; but hearts have been moved to feel for and assist us, in different tongues and places. The young Frenchman in Marseilles! The Arab Janisary in Egypt! In our last voyage, and suffering imprisonment in quarantine, Solomon, our Jewish friend, served us day and night, with the kindest attention! Also, in the most surprising manner, Capt. H——n of this vessel, rescued us from the greatest extremity! By sickness, we have several times been brought into imminent danger; but without a physician, the Lord has raised us up, and helped us thus far. I, therefore, still believe that he has a purpose in our journey, though undefined to us, and that he is determined to prove our obedience, and accomplish it. This persuasion is the more strengthened, because I know that I have no design of my own or desire to go, but to submit to Him, and fulfil his will, not knowing the things that shall befal me in the end.

Aug. 31.—Another day, and we hope to renew our journey; but difficulties increase in the way of poor and unaccustomed and feeble travellers, as we proceed. Difficulties of language, acquaintance with the manners and strange customs of the people, protection, conveyance, and travelling equipage, etc. Most travellers hire a dragoman, or agent, in Beyroot, to accompany and assist them in these necessities until they return. As we are unable to meet such an expense, and fearful of trusting any but God, we have been much in prayer respecting the uncertain prospect before us. But this morning, to our great joy, Mr. S——h, tne kind supercargo, and our friend Capt. H——n, and his lady, unexpectedly decided to leave their ship for a few days, and take the steamer, and go at the same time with us to Jerusalem.

Travellers at home will scarcely conceive how great a privilege their company will be to us here, and we receive

4

it as a peculiar and direct arrangement of love from God. How wonderful are all his ways! If their lovely child had lived, they could not have gone; also, during their visit of sorrow to Arbay, the missionaries became attached and interested for them, and sensible of Capt. H——'s generous and various donations, they are now assisting him in making the best arrangements for his short visit to Jerusalem! One of their former scholars, an Arab convert of intelligence, who is acquainted in Jerusalem, resides at Jaffa, as an agent for his brother, the American (Arab) Consul there. On account of his respect and obligations to the mission, they can command his attention and services, and have, therefore, written a letter for Capt. H——n to him, desiring him to accompany and assist him until his return.

Sept. 1.—All is bustle and preparation on board; the steward preparing cake and provisions for the way; the sail-maker making canvass saddle-bags to carry up the mountains, etc. The ladies of the mission have just sent one of their saddles for Mrs. H——n, as such a thing is not manufactured in this land, and cannot be obtained in Jaffa! They are indispensable to European women in ascending the rugged steeps before us, and I have made inquiry in Beyroot without success.

Sept. 3.—On board the "Grand Turk," a small English steamer, that during the last year has commenced carrying the mail from Egypt to Jaffa, Beyroot, and Smyrna once a month. Last evening we embarked with our American friends, whose kindness has truly endeared them to us; beside which Capt. H——n will receive no remuneration for our long stay with him. This is also a great help from the Lord, as our unexpected detention would have been very expensive on shore. We expect to reach Jaffa about ten o'clock this morning. The fare amounts to eight dollars in the first, and we pay six dollars in the second cabin. We had mattresses spread down under the awning, on the quarter-deck; several richly dressed Turkish passengers laid their mats near us; the moon shone brightly all night, and in our riding clothes, with umbrellas to shade our faces, we sought a little rest. In the morning the steward brought us a scanty and poor breakfast, which seemed a great change from our late excellent fare. Soon after an English lady came up from the first cabin, and began to converse with me respecting our near anticipations of landing in the country of Israel. She mentioned the difficulty of ascending the mountains, to which I responded by saying that I had reason to expect much suffering, as I had no saddle. She was surprised at this, and seemed much concerned for me, and immediately said, "It is not possible for you to proceed without; I have one with my baggage, which I will lend you, as I intend remaining some months in Jaffa, and shall have little need of it at present, and you may keep it, and use it, until you return." What was my surprise—if a sheet had been let down from heaven to my aid, as once it was in vision in this vicinity, it would scarcely have been more marvellous, or more timely, and helpful to my necessity! I find that my new friend is the devoted Mrs. W——, so long an approved missionary in India, who is on a visit of benevolent inquiry to Palestine. Again my faith is encouraged, that the Lord accepts my sacrifice, and will open all my way. Jaffa is in sight; several Arab boats are coming from shore to meet us, and I must drop my pencil, expecting soon to set my feet on this long-expected shore.

JERUSALEM, *Sept.* 5, 1849.—After a tedious journey of near four months, we arrived yesterday, about 11 o'clock, A. M., in this sacred city. In my relation, I will now return to our landing in Jaffa. This little city, is the only sea-port of Jerusalem. It is built on a small eminence, rising directly from the beach, which stretches low and sandy, each side, as far as the eye can reach. From the sea, its first appearance is somewhat like an immense beehive of small dome-roofed, clay-colored houses, with no trees, except two or three tall palms, in sight—as its rich and beautiful gardens are back of the city, on the receding plains. The surf here is constantly high, and there is no protection for shipping. As our long boat approached, on the top of bounding waves, the boatmen jumped into the water to their waists, to hold it from dashing against a projecting shelf, upon which stood a crowd of half-covered Arabs. We were all soon pulled up by our arms, and stood at length upon the soil of Palestine!

After pressing our way through men, donkeys, and camels, we were directed to the American Consul's, who received us with kind, yet mute attention. The letter from Arbay was delivered, and a messenger despatched in search of Mr. M., the educated brother of the Consul, who soon came and acted as an interpreter, and at once set about obtaining animals, etc., for our journey. Meanwhile we partook of a good Oriental dinner, provided by the Consul, who, with his beautiful young wife, and little son, were somewhat troubled with handling knives and forks, which were used on our account. About three o'clock, our baggage was bound with cords upon the backs of two mules, and committed to a muleteer, who drove them carefully before him. Our horses were saddled, and with Mr. M. before us, in single file, we were soon winding out through the narrow labyrinthian passages of the city. It is difficult to convey an idea of these Eastern cities, with their narrow crooked streets and alleys, and the manner in which their houses are built and joined, one into another irregularly. They have very low doors, but no windows, in the lower stories, and the houses appear like a rough continued wall, each side of the street, which winds every way to suit their location. Sometimes the passages are over-arched like railroad tunnels, with houses upon them. They use little wood in building, except for doors and window casings, and the roofs are of stone and plaster, and are necessarily arched like a dome.

We slowly crowded along, by loaded camels, mules, and donkeys, bearing heavy sacks, and flag baskets, of fruit, grain, charcoal, and various colored and strangely-dressed people, all wearing a scarlet cap, with a long blue tassel on the top, and flowing garments. A few wear only a short loose shirt, but generally they have a full skirt, confined at the knees, and bound around the waist with enormous girdles. Their complexions are usually quite dark, but their forms and features are often very fine. As we came out of Jaffa we passed the gardens, which are watered by primitive machinery, and contain a variety of fruits and vegetables—we saw oranges, lemons, dates, figs, pomegranates, grapes, and melons; and the prickly pear, which is used for hedges, grows here to the height of twenty feet, and the stalks are sometimes over two feet thick; its large thick leaves fold heavily and closely over each other, and are surrounded with orange-colored pears.

As we left the gardens, a wide plain opened before us, on every side, extending beyond our sight, rich and beautiful, with a slightly undulating surface. Here and there, in the distance, were small villages, or clusters of clay-colored fragments of walls, but I saw no isolated, or single dwelling by the way, or fenced divisions of the soil. Here first I saw large orchards of olives, which at a little distance appear like old apple trees. The foliage is dense, and the dark glossy leaf resembles the yellow willow in form, with the same silvery white on the underside, making their appearance beautiful when stirred by the wind. Our narrow path-like road, lay between large wheat and barley fields, which were irregularly joined with ploughed spaces, and turf land. Here a shepherd was following hundreds of white sheep, and black goats, feeding together, which was a fine illustration of our Saviour's parable, (Mat. xxv. 32;) and there a drove of small spotted cattle were lying down, and beyond, some camels were browsing from the high branches of trees! A missionary and his daughter, belonging to Jerusalem, a young Turk and some Arab travellers joined us at Jaffa, and our little caravan of about twenty animals were making all speed to reach a walled village, called Ramlah, (the ancient Arimathea,) which is situated half-way to the mountains, before dark.

Just before sunset, our horses, which were the poorest of the company, began to lag behind the rest, and despite of every effort to urge them forward, we were soon left out of sight. The way in some places was so indistinct, that I began to fear that we should mistake their track and be left to the mercy of the Arabs! We saw one on our right, with a long gun, approaching us, when suddenly our good friend, Capt. H——n came scouring back to our relief, and as he wheeled his horse, upon reaching us, his saddle gave way, and he fell to the ground! He was soon, however, mounted again, and the Arab passed in silence. With much difficulty he succeeded in driving our animals forward, until we reached the rest of the party, who had kindly waited for us. It was late when we reached the walls, and passed slowly one by one, into the close dark passages of Ramlah, turning to the right, and the left, and then forward, until we halted at a door on one side, and entered into a wide court, surrounded by kitchens, stables, etc. Here we alighted, and ascended a flight of stone steps into another court, from which opened large arched rooms, all of stone. It was an Armenian Convent, where Mr. M. informs us, they often lodge, but do not feed travellers, unless they have previous notice, as their native cooking is so different from Europeans. A dark turbaned man in loose garments, however, soon came in, and brought us some coffee without milk, in tiny cups, and a servant followed with a fine watermelon. The gentlemen had one room, and the ladies another, with mats and coarse cushions laid upon the floor round the sides of the room, where, being much fatigued with our new exercise, we were glad to lie down and rest.

Before one o'clock the moon was up, and the horses ready, and we set out towards the mountains; a number of natives joined us here, having small bells on their mules and donkeys, and we made quite a picturesque appearance, one by one, threading our way by moonlight. The country still continued plain and fertile, and we passed several threshing floors, with piles of wheat and chaff on the ground, and Arabs lying asleep, without blanket or pillows. Here and there were gardens of melons and cucumbers, inclosed with a few stones piled carelessly round them, and a little hut, or lodge in the centre. As we advanced, the soil became stony, and at daylight we reached the lower terrace of the mountains of Judea. In the grey dawn, the first appearance of these naked heights of rock, rising in solemn grandeur, so suddenly from the plain, much impressed me. They proved to be the out-post, and lower foundations of rock-embattled Zion. Their position and height, seem to defy the wisdom, or tool of man, to chisel even a pathway, but along the ravine, where the rain torrents of ages, has worn a rough causeway, there is room for one animal to climb at once, over the loose stones, gradually ascending, round and upward, from the base of one mountain to another, slowly gaining the sacred eminence, supposed to be about 3000 feet above the sea, on whose rugged platform stands JERUSALEM!

The first two hours we saw no trees, except in the ravines a few old olives, and in places some rough-leaved plants were clinging to the rocks, many of the mountains are circled with natural terraces, upward to their bald grey summits. As the sun rose the heat became intense, and the reflection from the lime stone cliffs was very oppressive. As we approached the city, there was more fertility; here and there we passed a wide valley, covered with fig trees, pomegranates, and vines, and on the larger terraces were vineyards, bending with fine grapes. Each little strip of soil, was inclosed with a rude stone wall, and a small tower in the midst with an Arab watching the grapes. The appearance of these mountains is unlike any that I have seen, and to me were awe-inspiring, as if the GREAT ARCHITECT of earth had with design heaped their naked piles, as invulnerable fortifications, to the place where He has chosen to place his NAME. We suffered much by the way from heat, and the great exertion of keeping our seats, in the rough and precipitous path, as the muleteers from behind would urge forward our weary animals. After slowly gaining one summit after another, we suddenly found ourselves on an extended table-like elevation, very rocky, but interspersed with olive trees. In the distance, towards the east, rose Mount Olivet! and facing it, on the west side, declined towards its base, the high grey walls, and domes, of JERUSALEM!

Our caravan paused in silence, and then a murmur rose, *Jerusalem! Jerusalem!* I had read so much of the sterility of its neighborhood, and its appearance of desolation, that my first feelings were those of happy surprise, to see thrifty olive trees, pomegranates, and figs in its vicinity. On the north, the foliage at this dry season of the year is deep green, and dense, and makes a beautiful contrast as the walls emerge beyond. The singular and unearth-like beauty, of its lone rock sentinelled SITUATIÓN, for a moment surpassed my early and sacred recollections of Scriptural delineation, while its formidable ancient walls and towers, its lofty minarets and domes, give it an air of peculiar solemnity and grandeur! Several Turkish soldiers, with polished weapons, bowed a silent welcome, as we entered the Jaffa Gate. The streets are narrow, and paved with heavy uneven stone, which are glossy by long use. During our ride I felt much concern how we should obtain comfortable accommodations with our moderate means, as Mr. M. informed us, that the charges were very high, at the only English hotel in the city. We, however, concluded to put up with our American friends during their short stay, in which time we hoped to make a more favorable arrangement.

After several turnings and windings, and ascents and descents, under the arched passages, we reached the hotel, but found only a porter, in a small room adjoining, who informed us that Mr Meshullam, the proprietor, was residing in Bethelehem with his family through the sickly months, and as it is not the season for travellers, the hotel was closed! From our long fast, and excessive fatigue, we were much exhausted, and our perplexity was extreme! Mr. M., however, feeling his responsibility to the American gentleman whom he had in charge, commanded the porter to send a messenger, and inform Mr. Meshullam, of the number and importance of the travellers who were waiting, and request his immediate attention. Here again, we acknowledge the peculiar mercy of the Lord, for had we arrived unattended by these friends, our peril and suffering must have been great, and we should not have met with our kind host. In about three hours he arrived, with his Greek cook, waiters, etc. The rooms (which are ancient dome-covered apartments, with plastered walls and floors,) were opened, and speedily put in neat order, and at four o'clock we sat down to dinner. We had good soup, a leg of roast mutton, potatoes, and tomatoes, (which Mr. Meshullam has recently succeeded in cultivating here,) excellent bread, some delicious grapes, and figs, freshly gathered, and wine from the vineyards of BETHLEHEM!

Sept. 8.—We have just parted with our kind friends, with emotions of the most sincere gratitude and esteem, and have sent back letters by them to our distant and beloved at home. We have found an unexpected friend in our host; he is a converted Jew, a gentleman of kind and affable manners, and treats us with much attention. He has made us a most generous and favorable offer of residing in his family, while they remain in Bethlehem, and afterwards at the hotel, until we leave Palestine; he also engages to defray all expenses, and conduct us to the Jordan, Hebron, and the few localities that we are bound in Spirit to visit; to permit one of his sons to be our interpreter, and to provide donkeys and a guide for us to ride out twice a week beside, and all this at a most reasonable charge. We would humbly recognize the hand of the Lord, in thus providing for our necessities, removing the formidable local obstacles in our way, and opening so favorable an opportunity in the society of a pious, intelligent and old resident, for prosecuting the important inquiries for which we came.

Early this morning, we made our first egress from the walls on donkeys, accompanied by Ahmud, an Arab servant. We went out the Damascus Gate, on the north, and followed round the walls eastward, over a rough, path-like road, worn in places through the rocks, by the long tread of ages. After passing the north-eastern angle of the walls, we entered the upper valley of the Kidron, which runs from the north, narrowing and deepening towards the south. In every direction the rocks and hills are variegated with clusters of olive trees and cultivated spots, with here and there a ruined tower, a broken wall, the fragments of a tomb, a cave, and a dry and deserted fountain, and every where the foot-prints of a buried race. On the east, between the walls and the valley, reaching to its declivity, are many rough slabs and stones, and plastered monuments, to mark the place of the innumerable dead. As we proceeded, the walls stood high and grey on our right, the valley declined on our left and beyond it, on the east rose the hallowed Mount of Olivet. Language cannot recall the deep and tender emotions of my soul, when first I gazed in near vicinity upon its rugged height. Its lone and frowning cliffs, still shaded here and there by the olive, the fig, and the pomegranate tree, brought back so vividly "THE MAN OF SORROWS," who so often sought to weep and pray among its sheltering solitudes.

When we had advanced about half-way along this eastern wall of the city, we came to St. Stephen's Gate, and followed the road that leads from it down into the valley. The track is worn to a glassy smoothness over the shelving rocks, and from the relative position of the ground and the adjacent scenes, it is probably the same that Jesus ascended on the night of his betrayal! As we descended we saw in the bottom of the vale, across the brook Kidron, a cluster of dark old olives, enclosed by a white plastered wall, which we knew without an interpreter to be *Gethsemane!* There are other trees of the same appearance scattered round, some nearer the dry stony channel of the brook, and others under the steep rocky acclivity of the Mount. Here I began to realize a certainty of being near the deep shelter of rocks and trees, where our suffering Lord once prostrated himself upon the ground, in that last dark night of sorrow! If there is any spot of earth that retains the foot-marks of Jesus, it is here! Here are the time-furrowed trunks of those hoary trees, the bare primeval rocks, unchiselled and unmoved by man, the native stony soil, the dry and pebbly bed of Kidron, and the natural precipitous ascent of Olivet beyond, with its difficult pathway, deep worn among the rocks by the long use of climbing feet.

Here in the deep shade of the valley we paused awhile, as the sun was rising above the highest point of Olivet, just over us, in the very place where we soon expect to see the rising glory of the Sun of Righteousness. (Zech. xiv. 4. We then followed the circuitous path at our left, which winds up to the summit, and halted in the shade of the Church of the Ascension, which occupies this interesting site. As we looked down, Jerusalem was spread out as a map before us. Just opposite stood the carved portals of the closed and silent gate, and within, upon the Temple ruins, rose the high grey dome of the Mosque of Omar; a number of other Turkish mosques and minarets, the Church of the Sepulchre, several convents, old citadels, towers, and dome-roofed houses, all of stone, rise one above another to the western wall. As we returned by another path, the view from a lower point below the church was more distinct and perfect, where the disciples might have easily referred to the "stones" of the buildings, and where our rejected Saviour could literally weep "OVER" Jerusalem, and rehearse the prophetic details of Matthew xxiv. and xxv.

Sept. 10.—Mr. Meshullam has gone to Bethlehem to make arrangements for us to join him there; meanwhile, two of his sons and a servant remain, with whom we are making little excursions about the city. We have just returned from Mount Zion, whose summit is outside; but near the walls, on their south-west extremity, an old pile of buildings, in possession of the Turks, covers the ancient site of David's palace and tomb. There is a considerable level on the summit around, where are many tombs, new and old, also a neat enclosure, built by Americans, which is used as a cemetery for European strangers. The soil is light and stony, and seems composed of dust and ruins.

The sides of the Mount towards the south and east are terraced and occupied with spots of cultivation and scattered olives, and the wider slopes are "ploughed as a field." (Micah. iii.) We saw squashes and cauliflowers growing, although this is the dry season, when little verdure is seen. A tender solemnity oppressed my spirit, and I could scarcely realize that this is "MOUNT ZION," which was once the scene of such magnificence and power; where

David, the sweet singer of Israel, *first* breathed those divine inspirations of prayer and song, which for so many centuries have been a balm and solace to the Church of God. All is lone and silent now, only as an occasional Arab with his heavy laden donkey winds along the terraced declivity, or some peasant woman, with baskets of grapes and figs upon their heads, or skins of water from Siloam's fountain far below, climb slowly to the gate. In the distance, across the valley, towards Bethlehem, a train of camels were noiselessly bearing along their heavy burdens, with their drivers slowly following, and here and there were shepherds with their flocks of sheep and goats upon the rocky hills.

Sept 11.—This morning we went early to the Church of the Sepulchre, which is interesting as the *oldest* building in the city, and is supposed to have been built by the mother of Constantine, in the proudest era of early nominal Christianity. The front is much defaced, but its heavy portals and fretted casements show something of its early splendor. A miniature marble temple, of beautiful proportions and chaste design, stands upon the pavement, directly under the dome, and is called *The Sepulchre!* Several immense candle-sticks of gold and of silver, with wax candles, stand near its door, and hanging lamps above are always burning; the church is decorated with many paintings, gilt angels, sainted figures, and nameless relics and appendages of outward worship. The Latin and Greek church are united in its possession. A deep sadness oppressed me, as I came out and sat down at the end of the large open court before it to sketch the front, which is the only ancient part that I could identify, as the inside is entirely covered with later designs; but a crowd of poor beggars pressed so upon me, that I was obliged to leave it unfinished.

The darkness and silence of the streets increases the awe that broods over these sombre walls at night, in this city without wheels. This stillness continues till midnight, when I am often awaked by a sullen jar that sounds like distant thunder, and grieve to think of the weakness, suffering, and toil which occasions it. It is the sound of countless rude mill-stones, which are here mostly turned by women, who nightly commence to grind about this time, and continue till morning; the labor is so heavy, that it is too great for their weak frames to endure in the heat of the day. I have made one effort, and could scarcely move one of their smallest stones. The process is so slow, that it generally takes a woman an hour for each member of her family!

BETHLEHEM, *Sept.* 13.—Yesterday, with Mrs. Meshullam (who kindly came in to accompany us,) and her sons and two servants, we set out about three o'clock for this place: some on horses, and some on donkeys, and a camel going before with mattresses, furniture, and baggage for us. We left the Jaffa Gate, and descended into the deep valley of Hinnom, and crossed over to the ascent beyond, and opposite to Mount Zion. The road then lay in a southerly direction across a level cultivated plain. About half-way, we passed the Convent of Elijah, which is surrounded by a dense grove of flourishing olives; and nearer to Bethlehem on our right, in a very rocky situation, rose a little stone chapel and dome, recently erected by a rich Israelite, (Sir M. M.,) over the site of Rachel's tomb, whither the Jews from the city sometimes come to worship. As we descended a rough path, the village of Bethlehem, with its fine convent walls, appeared on a distant hill. The view was beautiful and picturesque; the deep valley before Bethlehem is terraced, and covered with vines, pomegranate, and fig trees, and deep groves of olives are scattered on receding hills, with two other smaller villages nestled among their foliage. As we ascended the steep rocky sides of the hill, I thought of MARY, who once "went up," *to* " the city of David," over the same toilsome way! As we passed we saw Arab women and children gathering fruit, and men driving loaded camels and donkeys.

At length we entered the narrow passages, between small stone houses built in the side of the hill; in some they were grinding, in some weaving coarse cloth and in others making relics, weapons, etc., as they are mostly here employed in mechanical trades. We stopped at a low door, and stooping, entered a small court, and ascended a flight of rude time-worn steps, to the house of Meshullam. The situation is high, and a large arched window from its principal room, looks out over the deep valley below, presenting a scene of singular beauty; a large oaken table stands in the centre, a divan, chairs, and camp stools, neat white curtains, clean mats, boxes, bags and jars, containing flour, meal, fruits, oil, and honey, are arranged in the deep niches of the walls, being the productions of his farm —altogether, an unusual mixture of comfort and Oriental simplicity.

At tea, his third son, Petro, returned thanks, in a humble and solemn manner. We had excellent bread and honey, boiled rice, and goats' milk and tea. Two Arab women took a lantern, and led me into the court, and opened another door; here were horses and donkeys tied and feeding; but Ahmud hallooing pushed them aside for us to pass by to a flight of steps, which led to a little court or terrace above, from which opened my room; a little garden was on one side, and a vine with purple grapes hung over the door, and one window, with pots of bergamot, looking towards the valley. This was an addition recently built, which the women told me had never before been occupied; a clean mat had been spread upon the plastered floor, then a mattress, a stool, a tin pan, and a measure of water upon the deep sill of the window, and a bottle of water from the well-spring of Bethlehem. I felt most unworthy of "room" in such a comfortable "inn," when my blessed Master was laid in a manger, like those I passed below.

Sept. 14.—Last evening, near sunset, we visited the Convent, where the Latin, Armenian, and Greek Christians have each their apartments. The priests treated us very civilly, and showed the reputed place of the birth and manger of our blessed Saviour. It is situated in a dark vault beneath the church, where lamps are always burning. Notwithstanding the uncertainty that may rest on its definite locality, a peculiar awe and tenderness of soul affected me.

The Convent is a fine stone building, with several courts and corridors, and many comfortable chambers, a garden, and every convenience necessary for comfort and retirement. From the flat roof we had a fine view of the interesting country around Bethlehem. A bare gray mountain, shaped like a pyramid, (where is the cave of Adullam, the stronghold of David,) rises a few miles distant; in another direction, extends in nearer vicinity, "the Shepherd's Plain," and every where the rocky hills, and deep vallies, spotted with olive trees. Many of the inhabitants here have fine forms, good features, and fairer complexions than the common Arabs; but their apparel is simple and poor. They are mostly Latin and Greek Christians, and claim to be descendants of the Crusaders.

Sept. 16.—We are becoming much pleased with our kind host, and his interesting family. He seems to be an Israelite indeed. He is about fifty years of age; very intelligent and energetic, and his whole heart and hope is in the good of his poor brethren, and the restoration of Zion. His recent experiment in cultivation is the *first*, that has succeeded in this land by a Christian Jew, since the dispersion! He has a hired house here, that he occupies during the sickly months; but in the season of travellers, he is much engaged in Jerusalem. The heat is such, that we improve the morning or evening to ride, and yesterday, about three o'clock, Meshullam accompanied us with two of his children, to see his little farm. We first passed down the rough precipitous track, which leads from the mountain site of Bethlehem, (south-westward,) where clustering vines, and figs, and olives, spring from the rock-covered surface, across a narrow vale, and another hillside of broken ledges, and smooth worn limestone, into the valley of the Spring. Nothing can exceed the barrenness, of the rocky heights that rose each side, as our path wound up the narrow ravine, with the hot flint, rattling beneath our donkey's feet.

All at once, in a turn of the opening vista, a spot of the most living green, presented itself to our weary eyes, and soon after we came to the irrigated flats. Thrifty fig trees bending with fruit, were growing among the cliffs each side. Pomegranates, full of their scarlet apples were here and there on the terraces; and an orchard of peach trees were breaking beneath their ripening load, some were two years from the stone; also pear trees, of full size, which Mr. M. planted four years since; lemons, olives, and vines. Here were fields of tomatoes, ripe and ripening, and the leaves as green as with us in June; they have now been bearing six weeks, and will continue till November. We saw cauliflowers, beets, egg-plants, beans, onions, etc. There were two patches of Indian corn, of a small kind, just gathered; and he has wheat fields and a vineyard, further up the valley, beyond the Pools of Solomon. He has gathered out the stones, and made walls, enclosing the choicest part. The entire surface is irrigated by narrow channels round square beds, and I realized as never before, the beauty of the Scriptural comparison, "of a well watered garden," Isa. lviii. 11.

At length we reached the fountain, deep and cool, of the best water, which springs from the rock near the foot of the mountains at one side; while the ancient and well preserved aqueduct from the Pools, runs along near the summit, many feet above. I filled a bottle from the Spring, for the distant and loved, as I believe it is *the same* that the Son of Jesse, the Bethlehemite, so loved, in his youth, as there is no other such fountain or well near Bethlehem. Here I plucked, and ate, fresh figs, peaches, etc., in one of the vallies of Israel, reared by a CHRISTIAN ISRAELITE! He said, "If a few brethren of like precious faith, would come and unite with me to till this desolate land, and do good to Israel, it would be the happiest day of my life;" adding, "that there was sufficient land in the valley to support ten families, in love and happiness, if they were united to serve God!" We returned at sunset, greatly pleased with this specimen of the fertility of this deserted land.

Sept. 17.—Yesterday, after dinner, we rode out to see the Pools of Solomon, once called "Heshbon." Our course led over vallies and hills, covered with rocks, a perfect surface of crags; the path (for I cannot call it a road) is worn through beds of rock, to a glassy smoothness, which, as no wheels have ever passed, conveys an idea of great antiquity. Hills, bald and grey, and their eternal garniture of rocks, rise every where, summits of Zion's lower battlements, upheaving to the sky. These solemn, lone, and silent sentinels, greatly affect my soul, and the expression, "MY MOUNTAINS," by Jehovah, so oft repeated in the prophets, seem echoing among their solitudes. At length we came to the valley of the Pools, and the dark old walls of "Solomon's Castle," (Bath-rabbim) standing beside them. They are about forty feet high, and inclose a considerable square. There has been a tower at each corner, but they are fallen, and the inside is half filled with ruins. There is but one entrance, a low well secured door

A few yards beyond, is the first Pool; which is a deep reservoir, an elongated square, hewn out of the rock on one side and end, and completed with immense stones, covered with a cement, or plaster, which, though broken in places, continues, smooth and hard. A large fountain, near the door of the castle, is conducted into it under the ground. This upper Pool is nearly half full of water, at this dry season, when there has been no rain for the last five months. The water is very clear, though as it is never cleaned out, there are long green weeds growing at the bottom. A few rods below, in the descending bottom of the vale, is the second, very similar, with a little water; and still gently descending, a little further is the third and last.—This is empty, and I had a fine view of the interior, as my quiet donkey stood upon its brink. Terraces are cut in the sides, and a stair-case descends to the bottom, so the water could have been reached at any depth. The plaster in this is almost entire, of a lead color, beautiful and smooth, and still strangely defies the burning sun of this summer's sky, and the flooding rains of its winter!—Meshullam informed me, that the Pools are also fed from wells, some miles distant among the hills, and their subterranean passage among the rocks is still preserved!

The aqueduct, leading from them through Bethlehem to

Jerusalem, commences here, and winds along the side of the hill, above the valley, that rapidly deepens below the Pools. Its construction is most peculiar: a hollow tube, resembling our brown stone-ware, is laid a few inches beneath the surface of the ground, and a rude pavement of regular unhewn stone placed above. The stones are about three feet long, and half the width, and laid crossways, in a solid and close manner, over its entire course. Nothing which I have seen here, has so impressed me with a sense of the early wisdom and power of Israel, as these true remains of the Aqueduct and Pools of Solomon! As we returned, we followed the narrow path beside the Aqueduct, which winds along the dizzy verge of the hills above the cultivated vale, which we had visited before. It lies three-fourths of a mile below the Pools, and its loveliness was enhanced by the deep shade of the mountains, as we looked down from such a height upon its shadowy green. Here and there a stone has been removed, and a small aperture broken, by the Arabs, to water their flocks; but the water flows on, without serious obstruction, until it reaches Bethlehem, and is the chief supply of the village. Beyond this point it is broken, and fails before reaching Jerusalem.

Sept. 19.—Our friend has been ill for some days, and Mrs. M. is much afflicted on his account. Two of the children are unwell, and her health is delicate, and I have had an opportunity of sympathising with them in this hour of trial. Their isolated position, among uncivilized neighbors, with their young children, makes their case truly affecting.

Sept. 20.—M. is still much indisposed, though somewhat relieved. He converses freely with us of his early life, religious experience, and present peculiar position, and our interest and confidence in him is steadily increasing.

Two Germans, who had for two years been residing in Jerusalem, seeking an opportunity to occupy themselves in this land, have visited Mr. M. several times, since our stay in Bethlehem. They are anxious to enter his employ, that they may profit by his experience, which has proved so successful in his agricultural experiment in Artos for the last four or five years. His difficulties have been formidable, on account of want of suitable tools and seeds, and acquaintance with the various alterations of season, wet and dry, and the practical applications of modern tillage, with unaccustomed native help. These obstacles, however, by his perseverance and energy, with the Divine blessing, are rapidly disappearing. These Europeans are so greatly encouraged by his example, that they are making propositions to labor for him at Artos, without wages, that they may become initiated in so interesting and promising an occupation. To such terms he will not consent; but has generously offered them a share in the produce of the valley, and engaged one of them to commence labor the present autumn.

Sept. 24.—We waited some days, in hope that M. would sufficiently recover to accompany us, as he intended, on our journey to Hebron; but he remained too much indisposed. Some difficulties were in our way, and he felt much concerned to make the best arrangement for us. As it is now very sickly in Jerusalem, his eldest son, Elijah, is confined to the English Dispensary, where he has been very useful for some years. James, the second son, is just returned from school in London, and is not acquainted with the Arabic language, so that Petro, a lad of fourteen years, is our interpreter. Ahmud, an unaccustomed Arab, has been once there, and professed to know the way. There is but one family in Hebron who are accustomed to lodge strangers, and Ahmud knew nothing of their whereabouts. But notwithstanding the peril and uncertainty that threatened us, we set out on the 21st inst., about two o'clock in the afternoon.

Hebron is the most ancient city remaining upon the earth, situated in the plain of Mamre, where Abraham dwelt, and where is still the Cave of Machpelah, where he and his family are buried. Ahmud was well supplied by our kind hostess with cooked provisions, coffee, wine, etc., and several blankets to spread upon the ground, if we should find no lodgings. Petro was delighted with the privilege of going, as he had never seen the spot so revered by every true Israelite. Soon after leaving the village, I perceived that Ahmud's wide leathern girdle was adorned with two heavy pistols, which, without powder or ball, he had borrowed for the occasion, as he was afraid of hostile Arabs by the way, and wished to make some show of importance.

Our way led by the Pools, and thence over a succession of bare and rocky hills. We passed a valley where was an old fig tree, some herbage, and three wells, connected by subterranean channels with the Pools. The rough mountain distance of almost entire rocks which had thus been penetrated, reminded us again of the wisdom and power which God gave to Solomon. We cannot easily reckon by miles, for distance is still noted here by hours' and days' journeys. About five o'clock Ahmud began to fear that we should not reach the city before dark, and proposed that we should stop for the night at a small Arab village on a neighboring hill. I knew that this was his lack of courage, (as he was accustomed to see travellers well armed and attended in excursions through unfreqented parts of the country,) and that such a course would not be tolerable or safe. I replied, that our errand was important, and that we must by all means sleep in Hebron, and that he might hasten the animals, which, after some hesitation, he pressed forward at their utmost speed. A species of dwarf oak brushwood grew here and there among the rocks, and we passed a number of places where the Arabs were cutting and burning it into charcoal; but we saw no habitations, and the road seemed very desolate, as we met only an occasional Arab with his gun, and once a few camels, with their drivers, carrying grain.

As we approached Hebron, vegetation increased among the rocks, a few olive trees were upon the hills, and ploughed fields here and there in the vallies. Before sunset our road descended into a wide valley between high, rough walls, with a layer of dry thorns closely piled on their tops. Here, thus enclosed, were extensive vineyards bending with the finest grapes in the world; and pomegranates, figs, citrons, large quinces, and melons in a flourishing state; also we saw cultivated fields, with wells and fountains, and large flocks of sheep, and goats, and one drove of small-sized but well fed cattle. As the distance lengthened, and the sun was rapidly declining, I became very weary with our rapid ride and the quick gallop of my donkey steed; but my mind was more pressed with a solemn looking to God for help and guidance in our present extremity. To fail of reaching human thresholds before the darkness came on, would have been perilous; but still more to reach them, and not obtain a shelter, and be obliged to pass the night in the midnight of the dark passages, exposed to vermin, dogs, and the more hungry and designing outlaws.

At length, a little after sunset, we entered groves of very large olives, and in a picturesque valley between several hills, we found the dusky, irregular walls of Hebron. These partly consist of ruins, ancient buildings, and other more recent Turkish additions. The twilight was deepening under the old archways, and numbers of Arabs, men and boys, began to follow and press upon us, curious to see and watch our movements. Ahmud and Petro were both much troubled, and made fruitless inquiries for the hospitable Jew. It grew still darker, as Ahmud halted under an arch and gave his bridle to Petro, and was about leaving to seek a lodging for us among the Arabs; I thought of Abraham's servant (Genesis xxiv. 12;) and at this moment of desperate need, I cried to the same God, and turning to look back on account of a noise behind us, I saw standing at a little distance, beside a low door, a tall young man in Jewish costume. He had a fair and intelligent countenance, and I felt a strong impression to seek his aid, and urged Ahmud to go and inquire of him To this he was strangely opposed, as if a bewildered fear possessed him; but, after many earnest gestures and entreaties from Petro, he assented. The young man conversed with him awhile, looking earnestly at us, and then both disappeared in the door that closed behind them. We waited a long time in trembling suspense; when they returned, Ahmud was laughing for joy, and cried out to me,

Ti-ebe! Ti-ebe!" which is the Arabic for good! good! "We then dismounted, and followed through the door into a very narrow passage that wound about through many walls and doorways. We saw many Jews, old and young, in small cells and half subterranean rooms, who gazed at us with seeming surprise, and some bowed as we passed by them.

It had been a hot day, and the confined air in their close neighborhood was very impure. At length, however, we ascended a flight of broken stone-steps, and I was much relieved to leave the atmosphere below. Here our mute attendant led us into a pleasant room, opening into the air, and furnished with carpets and divans, where was seated his father, a venerable man with a white beard, and also his wife and children. They saluted us kindly, and expressed much regret that we could not converse; but I soon ascertained that they were the *same* family of whom Meshullam had spoken, and the only one who receive strangers! I was much affected at this manifest token of the constant aid and presence of the Lord. This family were formerly from Austria, and are of fairer complexion than is usual here, and are of good stature. Several others came in to see us, and I was much pleased with their graceful manners and costume. The women were gentle, and fine-looking. They informed me that there are four hundred Jews in Hebron, that they are very poor, and greatly oppressed, and often beaten by the Mussulmen.

We were then shown a very comfortable room for our accommodation. There were two windows opening into an orchard of olives; the walls were very old and low, terminating in a small dome above, and whitewashed clean and white. The stone floor was carpeted, and wide sacks of wool, two feet high, with clean white covers, were placed on all sides of the room, with many pillows of the same. These are a kind of divan, used alike for seats and beds. A lamp was suspended from the ceiling; it was a small glass bowl filled with olive oil, with a floating wick, and burned well all night. Ahmud made us some coffee, and brought in his stores, and we had supper on a low stool, the size of a large waiter, in Oriental style. They brought in some neat calico quilts, and we conversed a little through Petro, respecting the hope of Israel. Ahmud was much pleased with the permission to occupy a sack in one end of the room, and, with his outer garment wrapped closely around his face, soon forgot his late trials by the way. Poor Petro was so exhausted that he refused to eat, and also fell fast asleep, notwithstanding the numerous fleas and bugs that now issued from the clean-looking sacks, which, with musquitoes, proved truly distressing.

I cannot easily convey an idea of the solemn exercises of my soul through the silent watches of that night. The old sepulchral walls over my head, the window looking toward the Mount, above "the Cave," the glistening moonbeams clothing all in white, and thought's quick retrospect, retracing back through David's typical reign in Hebron, and still back, unweaving all the dim prophetic history of Mamre's plain, till one, "a stranger and sojourner," "removed his tent and came and dwelt in the plains of Mamre, which is Hebron, and built there an altar unto the Lord." And then "THE PROMISE" on that altar given—a presence filled me, and I realized that God was there;—the same, the faithful, true, and HOLY ONE, who first called Abraham, and sware unto him, in this place, to give to him and to his seed this land, from Egypt's river to Euphrates, for his inheritance, eternally and sure, and that "ALL the nations of the earth shall be blessed in him;" and as I prayed, I felt it was the same One Spirit that compelled our pilgrim feet to come from the far-off land of the setting sun, to worship at his forsaken altar here; I saw that his time to favor Zion is come, and that he will now set his hand a second time, to recover Israel; for he has "visited the Gentiles, to take out of them a people for his name," "as it is written, after this I will return, and WILL BUILD AGAIN the tabernacle of David, which IS fallen down, and I will build again the ruins thereof, and I will set it up that the *residue* of men might seek after the Lord, and all the Gentiles upon whom my name is called."

While I realized this truth, and the *certain* and speedy

accomplishment of the WORDS of God were written upon my heart, with a new and LIVING POWER, a sudden awe oppressed me, as if a cloud had filled the room; and then the low arched door seemed to unclose, and a reverend Sire of noble form and snowy beard, with Sarah's shade, his beautiful and loved, came in; and following, Isaac and Rebecca came; and last, came one that halted on his staff, (HE that prevailed with God,) with Leah and his Rachel at his side! and as they paused, and seemed to look on Ishmael's and Isaac's seed, and turned to us—a solemn, loving reverence, paralyzed my soul, in waiting silence; moveless my eyes were fixed, and then the sense of words breathed soft and low, came to my spirit's ear, "Thrice welcome, children of another fold, thrice welcome home!" and then in spiritual communion, I drank the sense of their rejoicing at the glory now soon to be fulfilled! But was this all a dream? Are there no sleepers in Machpelah's Cave? Will they not rise again, and soon walk forth in the sweet glory of eternal youth, when their now desert land "shall blossom as the rose," and become "like the garden of the Lord?"

The morning came, and Ahmud was soon ready with our coffee, etc., and we walked out with one of the sons of this family to see the city. The buildings are partially divided into two parts, one rising on the sides of the hill, where is the Cave of Machpelah, over which now stands a Turkish mosque, and the other part on the acclivity nearly opposite. In the level between is sunk a deep reservoir, which is filled in the rainy season, and supplies the inhabitants through most of the summer with water for common use; but their best water is brought in goat-skins from springs outside the town. We walked up a considerable ascent to the door of the mosque, which was guarded by several Turkish soldiers, as no Christian or Jew is permitted to enter. Notwithstanding the Jewish lad was protected by our company, the Arabs would scarcely let him pass without insult. We then followed a circuitous path, and climbed the steep hill above the mosque. After we emerged from the ruinous dwellings, the soil was cultivated, and a few olive trees were growing on the summit.

This city is the oldest of which we have any record; and we have no account of its having ever been entirely destroyed, so that there is no doubt respecting the true location of the tomb. As we stood on the summit, and overlooked the spot where lies Abraham and his family, the dense groves of old olives, and the dusky broken walls and ruins, a tender reverence filled my mind for the place of the repose of one who was called THE FRIEND OF GOD, and who gave his only son a sacrifice in proof of his LOVE! We then descended by another way, and passed through the bazaars. Here the narrow streets were mostly arched above, and on benches and stalls, on each side, were exposed for sale grain, fruit, fresh mutton, chickens, pigeons, eggs, etc. In the dim light through the narrow passages, loaded camels, mules, donkeys, and horses and their riders, in single file, were pressing slowly along, while those on foot were often obliged to lean against the stalls to avoid their trampling feet, being always advised by the careful halloo of the drivers. Sometimes their burdens were so enormous, as almost to obstruct the way, consisting of sacks of wool and charcoal, grain and lentiles, faggots of brushwood, and large baskets (suspended on each side of the animals,) of grapes, figs, pomegranates, melons, etc. There are also recesses in the walls, some ten feet square, in which are arranged many kinds of merchandise, dry goods, and groceries; and the seller, sitting in the midst, easily reaching all his goods to accommodate a customer standing in the street before him. The bazaars are similar in Beyroot, Jaffa, and Jerusalem. I purchased about four pounds of their large delicious grapes for ten paras, (one cent,) from which I selected a cluster, which, with a bottle of wine from our Jewish hostess, I preserved as a token from this place.

At ten o'clock we took our donkeys, and proceeded homeward by another route, that we might see an ancient oak, situated a little way out of the town, in a fruitful vineyard, now revered and celebrated as THE OAK under which was Abraham's tent, when the Lord visited him. When we reached it, I was surprised to find such a tree in this land, so destitute of forest trees, and I am assured that there is none like it in Palestine. It is very large at the base, and its trunk is wreathed and parted in four large divisions, spreading its dense foliage over a wide circle. The bark is rough and grey, and has the most time-worn appearance of any living substance that I ever saw. At noon it was ninety paces round its shadow; the leaves are very small and glossy, and appear like a species of the live oak; it is covered with beautiful acorns, with rough moss-like shells; its height is not very great, compared with its trunk and spreading boughs. Although the day was extremely hot, a cloak was necessary in the cool breeze under its shade. Here we had dinner, and fresh grapes from the vines, and excellent water from its ancient well. A living fountain or well, in September, indicates the location of ancient dwellings, as the modern possessors of this land dig no wells, and make no improvements. We know that the oak lives centuries, and the great scarcity of them here, which, with the vicinity of the tomb, at least justifies the thought, that if this is not the same tree mentioned by Josephus, it may be a seedling in its neighborhood.

As we returned I noticed several ruins, which were doubtless of Jewish origin. In one place immense stones were closely cemented in extensive walls and broken towers. In a beautiful but desolate valley there were several doors hewn in the solid rock, and near them were prostrate pillars, broken and worn. In another place were the remains of a house and an extensive court, and from among its large polished stones, which had fallen over it, issued a large fountain, where some Arab women were filling their goat-skins, and lading their donkeys, to carry to some of their mud-walled villages. We were faint and weary before we reached the Pools; and as we descended from the barren burning heights, and my eye rested on the deep blue reflected from the sky above upon their rippled surface, I realized the beauty of the metaphor of Solomon, (Song vii. 4.) Here we rested an hour, Ahmud made coffee, and we took a lunch in the Castle, seated on one of the ruined staircases that once led to each tower. There are still some low arched rooms remaining, (probably stables,) terraces, etc One fig-tree grew amid the ruins, and some Arab families reside here, who feed Meshullam's sheep and cattle, and watch his fields in this vicinity. While we sat there, several with their long guns, came in and saluted us; and a number of cattle and donkeys walked tamely in and out. These belonged to a child of Israel, and these servants were connected with his laboring household, and his efforts and success in such an interesting location, seemed, as I wept with the deep thoughts that pressed me, like the slender plant of restoration coming up among these ruins of Israel's former glory. Our animals being refreshed by the shade of the walls, and the water of the fountain, we proceeded, and slowly followed the aqueduct towards Bethlehem. Again we looked down upon the Eden Valley of the Spring, as the sinking sun was gleaming aslant between the mountains, upon its living green. The lights and shades upon its varied foliage enhanced its loveliness, and as it faded from my sight, I said, "Adieu! fair bud of promise, until we shall return, and all these desert hills 'shall blossom as the rose!'" We reached Bethlehem at sunset, where our kind friends received us with joy at our safe return, and with full hearts we returned thanks to God for his preserving love.

JERUSALEM, *Sept.* 26.—This is the 10th day of the 7th month, Jewish time—a day long to be revered by this poor heart of mine. We left Bethlehem yesterday, after dinner, with Mrs. M. and servants, to open the hotel. On our way, we again passed Rachel's solitary tomb, many camels and donkeys, returning from the city, and large flocks of goats, with a few sheep among them. At an old well near the road shepherds were drawing water, and their flocks were eagerly crowding round a stone trough to drink.

Evening.—This afternoon we visited seven synagogues, in which the Jews have been all day mourning. Each house was filled with men and boys, and the women were sitting on the stairs, windows, and door sills. The males had their heads covered, with a white worsted scarf, bordered with blue, and were chanting piteously, and moaning aloud, reading an entire volume of prayers, and ejaculatory complaints together, from sunrise till evening.— The faces of the women were exposed; but their persons were entirely wrapped in the universal white garment of this land. There were many very poor, and aged persons among them, and the scene was truly solemn, and affecting.

Oct. 5.—Again, dear friend, I resume my pen, to state that on the 27th of September, about one o'clock in the afternoon, we set out to visit the Jordan. But first, I must say, that it is a matter of no small importance, to make the necessary arrangements. Meshullam still continued too feeble, from his late illness, to accompany us, as he proposed, as it is the most unfavorable season, when few travellers risk the danger of fever in venturing through the heat. Three Shieks waited on M., and insisted on a large and customary tax to them, as they claimed to be proprietors of the territory over which we must pass, and also for hire for four Arab guides—(after receiving the money they sent only three!)—and their provisions, and expected buck-sheesh, or present. To this all travellers are still subject. Our host made the arrangement cheaper than usual; but, with our animals, etc., it cost him twenty-five dollars. It is usual to carry a tent; but as we proposed only a short visit, over one night, we decided to go without. We were supplied with carpets and blankets, provisions, coffee, wine, water, and even charcoal to kindle a fire, such is the desert road over which we must pass. I rode Mrs. M.'s large white donkey, an easy, gentle, creature, of great endurance, and with Ahmud and Petro, we set out in the heat of the day, as we rode out of the Damascus gate on the north, and followed the walls round eastward; we found that the power of the sun was very great, and there was a slight hot wind, called here sirocco, which is very oppressive. We crossed the valley of Kidron, by

Gethsemane, and passed over the southern extremity of Olivet, by a rocky path, to Bethany. One of the Arab guides stopped at the door of an old tomb, and plucked a twig from a small tree, and gave me; and I learned from Petro, that it was the Tomb of Lazarus!

Bethany is nestled on the steep declivity of the mount, south-east from Jerusalem. It has only a few poor stone houses, of a mud color, remaining, in which some Arabs reside. But my mind looked back to the sweet scenes of sacred Love, that were once enjoyed there, in the home of Mary, when our blessed Lord came in, weary from his temple labors, and sad, at the pharisaical darkness and pride, that opposed his mission of PEACE. Here in this humble secluded spot, he found welcome and rest; and here performed one of his greatest miracles. We passed onward, over steep precipitous hills, and deep vallies, now and then taking a parting glance at the lofty spires of Jerusalem, as they re-appeared between the receding heights. In the vallies were olive, fig, and apricot trees; but rocks succeeded to rocks, and as we advanced trees and vegetation disappeared. We soon perceived that our stony track was winding rapidly downward, threading one deep ravine after another, the high barren hills, steeply enclosing us. As the way opened, we still found ourselves on the top of high mountains, with still more steep and rapid descents.—Toward sunset, between distant peaks of Ash-like barrenness, we saw the wide Vale of the Jordan, and the Dead Sea, like a motionless pool of quick-silver, set in its arid expanse.

I have no language to describe this mountainous desert, without water, or tree, or shrub, or living thing, only as here and there the long grey lizard ran across the solitary path. The chalky cliffs, and limestone hills, glared fearfully beneath the fervid light, and the reflection burned the face as the mouth of a heated oven. I have read many descriptions, but had formed no correct idea of this rough desert scenery. In the deep chasms, where steeples would be lost, were wide beds of smooth washed stones, which seemed like the channels of mighty torrents, suddenly drained by some withering curse. Sometimes strata of varied colored rock, would assume the most fanciful architectural forms. From the smooth perpendicular heights of chalk, would jut out in bold relief, arches, and cornices, and domes, and pillars, with rude capitals, of dark red quartz; and some of the arches near the vallies were so perfect, that the chalk-like stone and earth from beneath had fallen out, forming a room and shelter from the sun. I thought, that thus the ancients might have found their first models for arches, fretted walls, and domes. I was surprised at the endurance of our poor animals, in climbing such steep rough crags, without water or rest, in the fearful heat. My donkey's little slender feet would cling to the crevices between the rocks, and then descending over some obstructing cliff, would slip, both fore feet down at once, so carefully, that I rode much of the time with the bridle loose upon his neck, and in all the way he did not once seriously slide or stumble! The sun set behind us, as we descended from the precipitous cliff of the last mountain, into the wide level of the Plains of Jericho. Here and there across its smooth turfless surface were interspersed small thick-leaved thorn trees, of a light and beautiful green. Our guides were civil and attentive, and scouted at a distance before, and at each side, to discover any hostile ambuscade. The principal was tall and erect, and a contrast to the red color of the others, being as black as velvet. With his long gun on his shoulder, as the darkness came on, he walked directly before us, and the others close in our rear. In about an hour, we came to a small stream of water! (a thing unseen before, since our landing at Jaffa,) which is supposed to proceed from the same fountain, which was once healed by Elisha. Here was a grove of large old fig-trees, and just beyond some ruins, called Jericho!

The moon had now risen, as our weary cavalcade, were saluted by the wild barking of the Arab dogs; and half-covered men, women, and children, came out of some hovels, among the ruins, and saluting our chief, said to us, Etfuddah! Etfuddah! (welcome, welcome!) After I alighted, they led me to their principal hut, which was enclosed by a wall some five feet high, and covered with a stack of dense thorns. It was dark inside, and they lighted a stick at a small fire of weeds at a little distance, and shewed me a corner inside. A large bullock shared one end, with chickens, donkeys, etc. The heat and smell was such that I came out, and chose a place on the ground, outside, and near the wall; but just as Ahmud was spreading down my carpet and cushion, the family camel came along, and crouched at my feet, claiming his better right. I was, however, soon accommodated near his side; while horses, donkeys, and dogs stood behind, and a circle of Arabs before me were sitting and smoking by the fire, and all gazing at the strangers. Petro had brought with him his favorite watch-dog, who now began to show his fidelity, by keeping their wolf-like whelps howling at a distance. He was very weary and thought, in return, that he must share one corner of my carpet; but his constant growl at every truant step, was tiresome to my aching head. Ahmud made coffee, and soon prepared a comfortable supper, which we shared, in a friendly way with our guides. Our neighbors were respectful, and sought in several little ways to shew us kindness. Their weapons, guns, and swords, were piled conveniently upon the ground, and some, alternately, patroled all night. As the moon ascended the light became so brilliant that our umbrellas were a great relief. Half reclining, in our dusty riding garments, in the close neighborhood of so many Arabs and animal fleas, we had no difficulty in keeping awake, to reflect upon our strange and interesting lodgings.

The Dead Sea lay in the distance before us, and in near vicinity was the Jordan, pouring its stormy tide into its dark and unhealed waters, at the base of the Moab mountains. The same blue depth, gleaming with its innumerable stars, and glorious moon, wheeled silently, above the same extended plain, where Joshua, Elijah, John, and JESUS, our blessed LORD, once moved, and acted out, the purposes of God. But now sad change, where once were cities, beautiful and strong, vineyards, and fruitful fields, and cultivated plains, thronging with busy life, and hearts that worshipped God, nought now remains, but the wild thorn, and desert soil, and heaps of ruins, scattered here and there, and the wild son of Ishmael master of the scene. The air was exceedingly hot and oppressive, and not the slightest zephyr curled the smoke of a fire, which an Arab woman sedulously replenished with the light thorn fuel, through the night, to drive away the cloud of musquitoes.

It has been estimated that this plain is 1,300 feet below the level of the Mediterranean, and that Mount Zion is 2,600 feet above Jaffa, so that we have descended about 3,900 feet! At three o'clock, when the moon was set, I lighted a taper and roused Ahmud, and desired that they would improve the time, before the sun was up, to reach Jordan. The guides told him that a hostile tribe was encamped near the river, and it would not be safe to go before light; but I feared the heat more, and urged them to venture. They then kindled a fire, as the poor woman and her infant had fallen asleep; and I watched their slow movements, as they poured some coarse flour, from a leather bag, into a wooden bowl, and kneaded a small cake, and raked the ashes smooth, and laid it in the fire. They watched it carefully, and turned it once, and in about half an hour, were ready to start.

Again on our donkeys, in single file, we followed their stealthy tread, while they required our entire silence, for their fear of being heard by the enemy. We proceeded toward the river over a level plain, of mellow soil, with only here or there a thorny shrub or tree, with the dark line of the mountains of Moab rising directly beyond it, the distance strangely lengthening as we rode. After two hours I perceived a sudden coolness in the air, and saw new shrubs, and then trees, and their foliage bending with dew! Soon after we saw a camp fire of the Bedouins, on the side of the mountain nearly opposite! and every attendant was so filled with apprehension, that they insisted on our immediate retreat. They said this tribe were more powerful and cruel than any other, and had recently proclaimed war with *their* Shieks, and that they would surely be killed if we were discovered. A strange courage possessed us, and I told them, we had travelled many a weary mile to visit Jordan, and we could not at this late hour give up our purpose, but that they should wait there, and we would proceed alone. To this they would not consent, but followed, trembling and murmuring as they went.

We descended one dry bank, and then another, and entered the dense thicket that fringes the course of the river, and heard the deep roar of its waters, but saw it not, till a moment more, when its torrent, shut within its narrowest banks, rushed wild and turbid at our feet! A shudder of surprise at the volume and rapid power of its deep current, was my first impression, as our animals halted upon its brink. Our guides now renewed their entreaties for our immediate return; and when they understood our design to bathe, they assured us of the greatest risk, as the current is stronger at this season than at any other. And Petro, also informed us, that every spring, at the usual time of bathing, some pilgrims were thus drowned. Seeing us still determined, they pulled us from our saddles, to hasten us, and tremblingly clutched their long guns, and peered in every direction through the thicket. Thick clusters of beautiful cedars, with their weeping foliage, shaded the water above the spot on which we stood, and beneath their covert we hastily changed our dress, and plunged into the stream, and were entirely immersed beneath its sacred flow. They were much alarmed, and one rushed down to the brink, expecting to see us carried away. But we were greatly refreshed by the sweet temperature of the water, and left it with regret, to resume our riding garments. We then secured two bottles of the stream, a few stones and plants; but seeing the terror of our dear young friend, after a short prayer, we tore ourselves away. We had intended taking breakfast here, and to have rested, and prayed awhile upon its lovely banks; but such were their earnest entreaties, we mounted our donkeys and looked back with tenderness, admiration and awe, upon its deep waters, and beautiful veil, of living green, as the sun was rising behind the dark cliffs of the Moab mountains.

Rapidly now we retraced our way, with the deep conviction, that Israel's cherished borders are still in the hands of the enemy. The sun was soon up, and the hot air scarcely moved the light foliage of the thorn, and we prepared our minds for a long fatiguing ride homewards. We re-passed Jericho, and an old stone building near it, where the Pasha keeps a few soldiers, and halted near the foot of the mountains for breakfast.

Soon after the fire was kindled, and the mat spread out, one of the Arabs gave an alarm! and descending from the mountains, we perceived a large company of Bedouins approaching us! Our insignificance in numbers, and appearance, dismounted, and suddenly surprised by such an array of barbarous men, for a moment appalled us! But soon recollecting the *Strength unseen*, which had preserved us through former perils, we calmly watched their long train, winding rapidly down the steep before us. There were about seventy-five camels, and as many mules, and donkeys, with their riders, who were bold looking and well-armed men. Our little company were all silent with fear, and stood motionless beside us. Their path lay within ten yards of the place where I sat, and our principal guide stood a little in the advance. A tall fierce-looking Shiek rode first, as their course depended on his example, I watched his motionless face as he came! He halted, and without speaking, reached out his hand for the pipe that was in the hand of our guide, which he smoked for a moment and then proceeded without breaking the march of the train behind. Our minds were solemnized with gratitude and praise to Him, who turneth the hearts of men whithersoever he will. They were a trading company, returning from Jerusalem, with their empty sacks, towards the desert beyond Jordan.

Soon after our coffee was ready, and as we were eating, a large drove of hungry hornets came and settled harmlessly on our napkins and plates, and we were obliged to retreat with a hasty supply. Here I considered the curse that still rests on the fair heritage of Jacob. The fountains and rivers have failed; the wells have been filled with stones, and lost; the sky is like brass, and the earth has become like ashes, from the prolonged heat. Israel said, "let his blood be upon us and our children," and crowned the "Prince of Peace," with "*thorns*." *Now*, you can scarcely pluck a twig, or flower, but it has a thorny stem. Wherever there is vegetation, thorns and briers spontaneously spring. At this destitute season of the year for plants, I saw many varieties, of trees and shrubs, that bore thorns! confirming the words of the prophet: "They have sown wheat, but shall reap thorns;" and "behold, I will hedge up thy way with thorns." But the promise to bless and restore this land, will as surely be fulfilled, when "there shall be no more any grieving thorn," and "instead of the thorn, shall come up the fig tree; and instead of the brier shall come up the myrtle tree, and it shall be to the Lord for a name, for an everlasting sign, that shall not be cut off."

Again, at ten o'clock, we resumed our journey, slowly climbing one barren ledge after another. The heat was unusually intense, and even the Arabs quailed beneath it; and before we had proceeded half the way towards the first mountain, their thirst was such that the goat skins were drained, from which I had frequently wet my head, face, and lips, and found great relief. After this our progress was slow, and the way lengthened wearily; the poor dog would thrust his nose in the shaded earth, under the edge of the rocks, and then closely follow under the shade of my large umbrella, and the animals were so overcome that the guides with difficulty drove them along. I began to feel a strange sickness come over me; my brain seemed on fire, and life and vitality were almost paralyzed. An Arab perceived it, and took a skin, and leaped away among the rocks, (as I afterwards learned,) to seek some water in a distant cave. They cheered my donkey onward, but in vain; and I looked till my eyes failed, but the water came not, and such was my agony that I began to suppose my case fatal. Several Arabs had been struck by the sun, a few days before, and died immediately, and my situation was similar. A little thorn bush cast a slight shadow, in one of the vallies, and I fain would have laid me there to die; but they urged me forward. Just then a slight breeze came through the deep gorge of the mountains, and I breathed again! Ahmud set up a piteous wail, and Petro said to me, "he is praying for you!" Poor Moslem! his pious sympathy revived my heart, and in a moment more, a shout was heard from the guides, "Moo-yah, Moo-yah!" (water, water!) and the Arab, with his wet black goat skin, came bounding down from the cliffs on our right!—He came, and filled my cup; I tasted, and bathed my head and face, while they all gathered around me, laughing for joy. I was instantly much relieved. After all had drank, and a hollow stone was filled for poor Tray, we urged the animals forward. I put my hand in my pocket, to reward the kind and thoughtful guide, and the rings of my purse scorched me! Another long hour, and we came to the first water, which is situated one hour from Bethany.—Ahmud hastened, and spread a carpet in the shade of the broken wall of the fountain, and laid me there. After taking a little wine and water, and bread, I was strengthened. It was a joy to see the poor animals drink, and I realized as never before, how great a blessing is *water!* In an hour we set forward; and at five o'clock passed Bethany, slowly descended Olivet, and reached the gates at sunset.

Oct. 6.—The next day after coming from the Jordan, I was nearly as well as usual, which much surprised our kind friends, as every one that has visited it this autumn has returned ill. With humble gratitude I would acknowledge the peculiar care of the Lord in my preservation. We have since witnessed "the waving of palms" in the Jewish Feast of Tabernacles, at one of their principal synagogues. They observe the feast in tabernacles, or booths, erected in the courts of their private houses. We were invited by one of their first families to visit them, they received us with much kindness, and showed us all over their house, which this week is arranged in their best order. Their rooms were comfortable and pleasant, with matting on the floors, divans with neat covers, beds, tables, and a few chairs, which they insisted on our using. Afterwards we sat awhile with them in their tabernacle, which was enclosed at the sides with curtains, and covered above with canes, and a few small pine branches, which had been brought from a great distance; a small table stood in the centre, upon which all their food must be eaten during this week of the feast; over it was suspended clusters of grapes, figs, and pomegranates. The aged father, with some difficulty, expressed that from sympathy he loved the stranger, especially Americans; that *his* people were free in *their* land, and he had known them in his intercourse of trade, in the Mediterranean, while he resided a long time in Gibraltar. He invited us to come often to see him, saying that "we are all united in worshiping the same God, and in looking for his kingdom." The mother and daughters were gaily dressed in English style, and served us with coffee, sweet cakes, and preserved citron, and showed us much love at parting. (We saw them several times afterward.) At the synagogue I was much affected at the attempted rejoicing of the poor, who went round in the procession, among those who carried palms, extending their hands for charity

I have forgotten before to state, that after our return from Bethlehem, we sought out our poor friend, Solomon, to whom we became so attached at the Qarantine. We found him ill with the ague, and in circumstances of great destitution. He was overjoyed to see us again, and this week of the feast is so much better, as to attend us in going and coming from the synagogues, and in our visit among the Jews.

Yesterday, with Solomon, we visited "the Mourning-place" of the Jews, where they go every Friday, to lament over a few remains of the Temple. It is a spot outside of the grounds, yet near the Mosque of Omar. There is a very high wall, the foundation or lower part of which consists of ancient stones of immense size, time-worn and defaced, yet each having the remains of a peculiar chiselled border. These are supposed to have belonged to the Temple, though composing part of a more recent structure. A few Jews were kneeling, with their faces against the wall; others were chanting in a sad, monotonous wail, while long weeds, creeping out from the crevices above, were hanging mournfully down over their bowed heads. Some women came, and bowing, kissed the stones; and every one took off their slippers as they approached the wall! The place accorded with my heart, and I sat down on the smooth worn stones, and bowed my head with theirs, and prayed that the King and Saviour of the Jews would soon "return, and build again the tabernacle of David, that has fallen down."

Oct. 7.—Last evening before sunset, (the time of our accustomed walk,) we passed out of St. Stephen's Gate, a little beyond which, it is said, that he was stoned, on the brow of the hill overlooking Gethsemane, and beside the path that leads down to the Garden. But we now turned to the right, and followed in the shade of the wall, through a closely-filled Turkish cemetery, to the Golden Gate. On each side in its neighborhood, the base of the wall is laid with the same kind of immense and ancient stones, that we had seen at "the Mourning-place." The portals and cornice of the gateway is beautifully carved, with chaplets of curious leaves, half-way resembling the acanthus and thistle. The entrance is twenty-one paces in width, and is closed up with smooth square stones of modern date, according to the prophetic word! (See Ezekiel xliv. 1, 3.) From this point there is a view, at once the most solemn and interesting; directly opposite, towards the east, rises Mount Olivet; and below, in the valley between, lies Gethsemane; while the deep sepulchral chasm of Jehosaphat extends southward, with its multitudinous graves, in minute prospect.

Oct. 9.—Yesterday was the last great day of the feast, and we attended, morning and evening. The Jews were gaily dressed in their best garments. The walls of the synagogues were decorated for the occasion with many pieces of rich embroidery. In blue and gold, and in white and silver, were wrought designs of the tables of the Ten Commandments, seven-branched candlesticks, and fragments of the temple and tabernacle service. Their pulpit is a circular platform in the centre of the house, surrounded by a balustrade, and many little hanging lamps of glass On one side, by the wall, is something like a canopied altar, from whence the priests took out some ten or twelve wooden cylinders, which are about one foot in diameter, and two and a half in length. These enclose copies of the Law, and are richly covered with tinseled silk of various colors, and have a silver rod attached to one end, with pomegranates and bells; then every male, old and young, took them in their arms by turns, and made a procession round the synagogue, singing and leaping, and shaking the bells, while numbers of the priests and others danced, and exulted before them, clapping their hands, and praising God, with portions of the Psalms. Every one present crowded near the aisles, to touch the cylinders, and kiss their hands as they passed. Only few of the women nearest the entrance could gain the privilege, and were often frowned upon, and rudely pushed back by the men, and aged grandmothers were thus insolently repelled by lads of ten years! If some young mother held in her arms a male infant, much decorated, she was permitted to press in a little, and put her child's hand upon the beautiful tinkling pageant. Fathers also took their sons of three and four years old in their arms, with the Law, and followed round, thus so early teaching them to help in the ceremony, and join in worship. Half of the procession were lads, from eight to sixteen years old, who, in their zeal to have the longest turn, would often strive, and even strike each other! The procession passed round seven times, with great noise; the Law was then returned to its place, and the congregation retired.

During the ceremony, those unoccupied were laughing and talking, standing, and pressing here and there irregularly. Some were much more engaged than others, leaping like David, with all their might, and others, each side, sprinkled rose-water upon them as they passed. Solomon appears very devout, and is much pleased with our interest in their worship. Last evening he carried a lantern for us, as the passages are entirely dark through the city at night, for every stall is closed, and windows rarely open into the street.

The rabbies have treated us with kind attention, and yesterday compelled us to sit in their pulpit, that we might have a better view of the ceremony. Some of the rich displayed much in their dresses, jewelry, etc.; while mixing with them, side by side, were some scarcely covered with ragged and filthy garments; and there was among them a great variety of color and feature. I cannot easily express the tender emotions of sorrow and reverence that oppressed me, while witnessing the ceremonies of this feast, which are here celebrated by the remnant of Jehovah's ancient and chosen people, on this ruined altar, in "THE PLACE OF THE NAME OF THE LORD OF HOSTS," still clinging, as through so many weary centuries they have done, to these types of unfulfilled promises, and still engraving them upon the hearts of their infant sons, despite their low estate and long captivity. This practice, of so early engaging their children in the active service of the sanctuary, is a pleasing contrast to the distance prescribed for the young by some of the Gentile sects. We understand by this how the children were in the Temple, ready to be witnesses for Jesus, by "crying Hosannah!" etc. I pointed an aged man, who was conversing with me, to the embroidered crown of gold above the Law, and signified to him that Messiah's REIGN was near, with which he was much pleased; and another said, "This is the *Father religion!*" But, while the multitude shouted so loud that we could not hear each other, I also praised MY Redeemer, "the King of the Jews."

Oct 10.—Last evening, in company with Elijah and James,) the eldest sons of Meshullam,) we walked out of the Damascus Gate, to what tradition calls "the Grotto of Jeremiah." It appears like a natural chamber, formed in the perpendicular side of an immense rock, which rises at a little distance from the walls, on the north side of the city. The entrance is some fifty feet from the ground below it, and yet it is approached from the hill, at the side, by a very narrow terrace. Here, it is said, in view of the city, that Jeremiah wrote his Lamentations over it. Beneath this aperture opens a deep cavern under the rock, in which is the supposed pit where he was incarcerated. At its mouth are some olives, and a fine lemon tree, growing, as it were, in the court of entrance. Here an Arab Shiek has a rude hut beside the rock; and as we looked down from the shelving terrace above, he and his donkey seemed small in the solemn depth. We then extended our walk through a grove of olives to a mill, where the oil is pressed. It was a clumsy attempt at machinery. Near it we saw a pine, lofty and flourishing, of the largest size of any tree in the vicinity of Jerusalem.

Near the walls of the city, we saw several deep excavations, cells, and subterranean rooms, with their arched roofs broken in, forming dangerous pits; also a dry reservoir of a lost fountain, with its beautifully carved trough, recently broken. Elijah said that it was entire a year since, but had thus been wantonly destroyed by the Arabs! In a number of places, we saw remains of the ancient walls, parallel with, but distant from, the present walls of the city, enclosing a much larger area. At every step, I was reminded that we were treading upon the records of buried ages. There are many tombs, in every direction, most of which are modern, and rude efforts of masonry. The present inhabitants, in burying their dead, excavate a square pit, in which, without a coffin, they unceremoniously deposit the body, in its usual dress. It is sometimes wound up in an outer garment, or sheet, and laid down horizontally, but more frequently otherwise, in any accidental position. The north side of the city is more easily approached than any other, being an undulating level, broken here and there by abrupt cliffs, between cultivated plats of stony soil, and thickly studded with flourishing olives. Hence it is from this side invasions have ever been effected. After the rain commences in November I am assured, that grass and aromatic plants and flowers, in magical beauty, spring forth and cover the surface, that now appears like ashy and turfless soil.

Oct. 11.—Elijah is engaged in the Dispensary of the

English Mission, until four o'clock, P. M.; after which, with his brothers, James and Petro, he accompanied us this afternoon to "the Tombs of the Kings," which are situated about three-fourths of a mile north of the city, on the way to Damascus. In a rocky plain, interspersed with olives, near the road, we found a square area, of perhaps one-fourth of an acre, sunk, and mostly hewn out of the solid rock, about the depth of eighteen feet. The surface of the earth around it is level with the edge of the sunken area, except on one side; it is excavated without, leaving a wall of the same rock, through which is cut an arched opening about three feet high. Through this we crept into the square, where was an old olive tree, some piles of rubbish, and broken slabs, etc. We passed through to the western side, where opens a portico, cut out, with steps descending beneath its roof, of stone. Its front above is carved, in beautiful designs, of curious foliage and fruit. No pillars remain, yet their fragments may lie buried beneath the hill of broken stone and earth, that half obstructs the entrance.

Under this portico, some feet below the level of the open court, opens a low and narrow aperture, through which, with lighted candles, we with difficulty crept. We found ourselves at once in a room about twenty feet square, and the dark chiselled ceiling some twelve feet above us. From this, through the same kind of narrow doors, opened three other similar rooms. From these again, other narrow doors opened into small closets, where there were shelves of sufficient size to hold large coffins. I examined the wall on every side with a good light, to find some fissure or seam in the rock, but it was every where the same, hewn out of the one entire hill of stone. Near by each aperture lay fragments of their doors, smoothly polished and chafed with bevelled edges; some were nearly entire, as they had been thrown down by some powerful invader! In the stone-wrought casements were grooves, and at the corner of the doors were hinge-like pins to fit, so that they could swing with perfect ease and security. There were also stair-cases leading down to an under-story of apartments, containing similar rooms and recesses. I was forced to the conviction, by the entire oneness of the rock, and by the appropriate but empty shelves, that this was indeed the tomb and power of royalty; that during the many contests of various nations and sects, which came to invade and destroy, with bigoted zeal; (these tombs being outside of the city and unprotected,) the sarcophagi have been all long since removed and destroyed, and their bones scattered to the winds. It is written, (Jer. viii. 1, 2;) "They shall bring out the bones of the kings of Judah, and the bones of his princes, and the bones of his priests, and the bones of his prophets, and the bones of the inhabitants of Jerusalem out of their graves, and they shall spread them before the sun," etc. This supposes sepulchres, from which they could *bring them out;* and in no way could these massive doors be thus mutilated and thrown down, but by determined enemies. The air within was close and damp, and I felt a sense of oppression, from the "darkness that might be *felt.*" As we returned, the cool soft air was a sweet relief, and we reached the gate in time to enter, with a fine relish for our cup of tea and cheerful lodgings.

Oct. 13.—Last evening we walked out of the Jaffa Gate, which opens on the edge of the hill, above the Valley of Hinnom. We descended into its stony depth, among the old olives, and took a seat on a rock among the thorns, that half cover the surface of the soil. The recollections of its dark history of blood and fire, cast a deeper gloom upon its present desolation. The walls on this side of the city are more regular and beautiful than elsewhere; and the tower of an ancient citadel of great strength, still remains in a good state of preservation, near the gate.

This morning we rose early, and desiring to spend a season in prayer on the summit of Olivet, before the heat of the day, we passed out of St. Stephen's Gate, and followed the worn furrow, down the rocky declivity to the Garden below. We passed by its hoary trees, as the burning glory of the sun was beaming behind the summit of Olivet; and as we paused, I thought how like our spiritual state was that speaking landscape. Gethsemane, in the deep shade of the Mount, is like our present pilgrimage of tears! while the bright rays of the rising sun, gleaming from behind its summit, was like our "blessed hope" of the near coming of the Sun of Righteousness! The mountain is a range of three summits, or elevations, the highest and central point is directly over the Garden, opposite and fronting the Golden Gate, and the site of the Temple. On this is now situated a cluster of walls and buildings, called the Church of the Ascension, where a family of Latin priests reside. The other two are unoccupied open fields, spotted with olive trees. Of three diverging roads, we chose the middle and steepest path, winding among the rocks and craggy trees to the right, across the peak, towards Bethany. There was a sweet cool air from the north-west, and the early dew gave a freshness to the deep green of the trees; the stony track was very rough and steep, and I was often obliged to sit down to rest, and was much affected with the thought, how often the Lord Jesus had climbed that rugged ascent, in the same direction, "TOWARDS BETHANY!"

When we gained the point to which our minds had been directed, the view was wide, and the most affecting to me of any that earth can give! Here JERUSALEM lay at our feet as a map; and the beautiful broad level of the Temple site, encircled with trees and fountains; and still above on its left, the lofty terraces of Zion, with the sealed gate, in silent reverence waiting, till He whose right it is to reign, shall come and open its long untrodden threshold. Not an Arab crossed our way, and all around the silent lonely hills kept Sabbath with us: a sacred presence seemed to rest upon the Mount, and I was filled with awe, and lifted up my hands with streaming eyes, and prayed that HE would quickly come, our long expected, and stand again on Olivet, (Zech. xiv. 4,) restore his heritage, and from the four winds bring his scattered and his waiting saints; and then we fell upon our knees, and plead the everlasting covenant of God with ransomed man; that for the name of JESUS, his alone-begotten, and for his kingdom's sake, and for Jehovah's Name, and truth, and promise sake, that he would bring again the long captivity of Israel, and build again his house of prayer, and set on Zion's hill, the King of Righteousness! And while we prayed, a cloud of blessing came, which words may not describe; for in a moment, to my quickened sense, the heap of ruinous rubbish, and the Moslem's shrine, was seen no more, and on its site a city, pure and beautiful, arose; and in the midst, in glorious majesty, the King of Righteousness, supremely reigned; and all the hills around, in Eden loveliness, spread out, an undulating plain! And then in shadow passed, the finale of this waiting hour, its trial, darkness, and its quick reward—"the COMING," and the REIGN of peace. But more of this anticipating faith I may not speak, but tears fell fast and free; my heart was strengthened in its sacrifice and purpose still to venture, in the path of faith, and hope unto THE END.

Oct. 14.—Some days since, we obtained permission of the Latin Convent, through our young friend, Elijah, to enter the enclosure of Gethsemane. They have recently purchased this privilege from the Turks, and enclosed eight of the most ancient trees, in the depth of the valley, where tradition marks the place where our blessed Lord sweat drops of blood. The wall is some fourteen feet high, and composed of whitish chalk-looking stones and mortar. We passed over the dry channel of the brook Kidron; Elijah knocked at the low door, and it was opened by an aged pilgrim, who acts as keeper and gardener. Here I was more sensibly affected than at any other of the marble-covered and cherished localities. The native earth and stones were bare and grey; the ragged time-worn trunks of the hoary trees, like solemn witnesses stood there, with their thin foliage, bearing olives still. I sat upon the ground beneath their thickest shade, and while the others were busy with the good old man, in a distant corner, where he was showing what he supposed were marks of blood upon the rocks, I fell upon my face and kissed the dust, and found a blessing there, in pleading all my cherished names of Christian LOVE; that for that blood and agony, we might be sanctified, and brought into his place of rest.

The gardener permitted me to take a small branch, with leaves, and a cluster of olives; and as we turned to leave, I offered him the usual present, that in this country is often claimed without pretext, but he steadily refused it, saying, in Arabic, that it was recompense enough for him to have the care of such a place! I was moved at this return, and laid my hand upon his breast, and looked up, while he united in the expression that our God would bless both him and us, poor pilgrims by the way.

Oct. 15.—We rose early this morning, and set out to visit "the Pool of Siloam." We passed the Turkish sentinels at St. Stephen's Gate, who stand in silence, and bow respectfully, as we daily go in and out, and followed the path southward, near the walls, by the Beautiful Gate, and descended into the Valley of Kidron, by an inclined path, below Gethsemane, and reached its depth by the time-worn Pillar of Absalom. Many small stones were heaped at its base, thrown here by the passing Jews, as a mark of contempt for that rebellious son. Here the hills nearly meet, and the ravine between them is deep and narrow, and the Valley of Jehoshaphat begins to open. On the side of the hill, opposite to the city, below the Pillar, is a solid ledge of rocks overhanging the path, in which are hewn several doors and tombs. The entrance of one has fine pillars of the same rock, and another at its side is cut out entire, in the form of a solid square, with a pyramidal roof, which is called "the Tomb of Zachariah." Here we paused, and remembered his prophetic testimony respecting the final restoration of Jerusalem.

As we followed the dry stony channel of the brook, the valley spread out before us, and was entirely covered with small rude stones, some two feet long; Hebrew characters were dimly visible upon them, to mark the place of the countless sleepers there! They were crowded together on the side of the precipitous hills, and extended into the narrow footway on the edge of the gullied chasm of the brook, which still descended, until Mount Zion, and a corner of the wall of the city, rose bold and high over our heads. Here again the valley contracted, and on our left commenced another range of lofty crags, with many square apertures, doors, and tombs, hewn out between their fissures, among which is nestled above, the Arab "village of Siloam," with their rude additions, in which their dogs and donkeys share with them the same shelter. Women were coming up from the fountain, some distance below, with heavy water-pots upon their heads, while men, with their long pipes, were crouched upon the overjutting cliffs, many feet above us, watching our progress. A little farther, we saw some mulberry trees, cultivated plats of ground, and thrifty fig-trees. On our right, water was issuing from the rock, by a narrow channel, irrigating the soil. This we afterwards learned, was a subterranean aqueduct from the fountain, cut through the rock under the base of Mount Zion!

As we proceeded, a ledge of rocks rose between us and Mount Zion; on our left were cultivated plats of beets and cauliflowers. At length this ledge abruptly ended, and from between it and Zion came out a large stream of water, rippling over the stones. Here were some eight or ten men, women, and children, with their dogs and donkeys, some getting water, and others washing their clothes, by rubbing them on the stones under the waterfall. They received us civilly, and an old woman, leading a little child, undertook to be our guide to the fountain. She led us back, round the end of the ledge, between the rocks and the Mount, where we found the Pool, or Fountain of Siloam, flowing from the base of Zion. The water issues from beneath an archway of overhanging rock, into a sunken reservoir. We descended the broken steps, under its cool shade, and drank, and bathed our head and "eyes," praying much that we might also be inwardly washed, and our eyes opened, as one of old, to see the perfect will of God. As we returned, and slowly climbed towards the gate, the sun had risen in its strength, and the deep shade of the streets proved a timely refuge from its power.

Oct. 20.—To-day is the holy Sabbath, when we know that our beloved household of faith, at home, will especially remember us in prayer. We rose early, and before breakfast, walked out of the Damascus Gate to the "Grotto of Jeremiah," and entered by its dizzy terrace into the chamber over the cavern. In the distance some Arabs were gathering olives, and some were passing towards the gate with skins of water. The soft air outside the walls was fresh and pure, and the cave afforded a cool shelter from the sun. Here we sung a hymn, and knelt and worshipped, and felt a spirit of supplication for the desolations of Zion; her scattered and oppressed children, and the sympathizing Christian remnant at home, and experienced a precious season of inward blessing.

Oct. 21.—The deep blue vault, and glorious ever shining sun is veiled to-day with thin grey-clouds, which is a delightful change and relief, after the long-continued brightness. Our poor friend, Solomon, has the chills again, and is unable as usual to come and see us; so in company with his brother, a young lad, we went to the Jewish Quarter, and passed from one narrow filthy passage to another, where we saw many poor Jews in circumstances of squalid poverty! Here and there we met a miserable donkey, with a few greens, or a little charcoal for sale, and the passage between the high rough walls, was so narrow, that the driver was obliged to press the little animal close to one side, that I might barely slip by him.

At length we entered a forlorn court, with old mats, and torn quilts, spread on one side by the wall for beds and divans, without a stool or table, or any furniture, excepting a few earthen dishes and jugs for water. I understood from the women that this was the common home of numbers of the poor. When the lad sought for Solomon, he was too ill to rise, and they led us down, through broken arches, and stair-ways, until we found him, lying with one mat and quilt between him and the stone floor, and an old blanket wrapped round him, without pillow or sheet! A small bundle and a basket stood in one corner, and an earthen bottle of water, and some black crusts of Arab bread near his head, were all his miserable store! He was much affected at seeing us, clinging to our hands, and kissing them with tears! We had interceded with the Hospital proprietors to shelter him, but they were full, yet Elijah had obtained some medicine for him, that stood near him, on the floor. He strove to tell us his misery, saying "lah kiwah! lah russ!" (no coffee! no rice! etc.) We had brought a few things for him, which with an additional mite, he received with many thanks. But oh, how our hearts melted, as we knelt beside him, that our poor relief could not reach his need, and with earnest prayer, we commended him to the God and Father of *Israel*. As we came away we met a rich and learned Jew, who had shewn us kind attention; we plead his poor brother's case; but he said, "Oh, there are so many just like him," and then repeated the story of their general destitution.

Oct. 22.—This afternoon Elijah accompanied us on a visit to the Armenian Convent, which is situated on the elevated ground near Zion's Gate. It is a fine large building, well endowed, and its church is richly decorated, and contains a great display of gold and silver, paintings, lamps, etc. The courts, garden, entrance, and the street near it, is very clean, and kept in fine order, and has the appearance of more comfort and elegance, than any thing that I have seen in this country. The Greeks and Latins have also a convent within the walls, which we have not visited. We have been informed, that the Greek Convent, though well established and protected by Russia, is not as fine, and the Latin is still more inconsiderable. The English Mission have an elegant church, recently erected, on a part of Mount Zion, which is within the walls, and near the Jaffa Gate. They have a Bishop, and several clergymen, and other members of the Mission residing here. On Sunday morning they have an English service, and German and Hebrew afterwards. We have attended several times. They have an English school for children, taught by a lady, and also a higher institution for converted Jews.

They have also a well conducted Hospital and Dispensary, where Jews are employed, and the sick are well provided and nursed, free of charge. A physician is in attendance, and medicine is supplied to general applications gratis. This branch of their benevolence is often improved by Mussulmen and others.

After leaving the Convent we passed out of Zion's Gate, which leads directly to the Tomb of David, which is situated on its summit, a short distance from the walls. We walked awhile upon its lonely terraces, from which we had an extensive view, of the surrounding country. As we returned we saw a company of lepers seated on the ground, who held up their maimed and decayed limbs, to excite our compassion, and the sight was most distressing, as we ventured near, to throw a few piastres among them. We then came through the Jewish Quarter, and were greatly afflicted with the abject misery of the poor residents. No description can equal the stern reality of their suffering.

Oct. 23.—My beloved friend, you will doubtless desire to know something of my experience, as to the spiritual result of my present pilgrimage of faith! Of this I would not speak prematurely, but providential incidents of peculiar interest and importance, attended by strong convictions of the Spirit, respecting unfulfilled *promises* to Israel have, during our short stay in the Holy Land, opened a new and unexpected field of duty and blessing to my anticipations of faith. You will then bear with me while I open this result, in the same way that my daily experience has, thus far, confirmed the truth to my own mind. When we first arrived, my desire was to remain as short a time as possible, supposing that my sacrifice and duty was completed by simple obedience to the mind of the Lord, in this consummation of my journey. We have, therefore, made it a subject of constant prayer that our course might be entirely directed of Him, and that his providence might open whatever duty or light, connected with Israel, there might be for us here. Our want of language seemed, to my unbelief, an entire barrier to all investigation, or personal communication, and I was necessarily driven more entirely to the Lord.

Through our connection with Solomon, we became familiar with the piety, doubtful expectations, and suffering circumstances of the poor, and found, by experience, that by approaching them with humble, loving confidence, their hearts are open to a righteous influence. By coming in obedience to our inward Teacher, against our own wisdom, in the hot and sickly season, when other travellers rarely risk the exposure, it has cost us much suffering and reproof from observers, but it has proved to be the most favorable season for our object, for it is the only time that Meshullam has leisure, or could have spared room for our accommodation, for so long a stay, even at double the expense! Through the temporary failure of his general health, at *this point*, he was hindered from his constant active engagements, and confined to the solitude of his summer house in Bethlehem. Our interest and sympathy in his peculiar position here met a reciprocal Christian response, and through this familiar connection with him and his interesting family, in the chastened feelings of this crisis, he opened to us, in different conversations, the details of his interesting history and experience, little deeming the impression it made upon our hearts, and the influence it would finally extend to others who are devoted to the good of Israel. His character, and wonderful experiment in agriculture, at this moment of dispensational expectation, when the Jews in every land are rising from their captive state, has greatly interested, and led us earnestly to consider the Lord's *purpose* in his sustainment.

He is obliged to be at Artos a part of the time, and for several days has been much occupied in giving directions to the young German, who is commencing to labor there. Although his new assistant is well furnished with means, and has engaged to board and provide for himself, M. is gratuitously making every provision in his power for his comfort. He has carried out his best tent for his use, and often sends his meals, cooked from the hotel. Such is his kindly care for the good of those around him.

Oct. 24.—As the time approaches for us to leave Jerusalem my mind is much exercised with regard to returning by the way of England. Before leaving America, this was my anticipated duty; but since our time is so near exhausted, I have prayed much that we may be free to return directly from the Mediterranean, and escape the long winter voyage northward. We have no acquaintance or introduction to believers there, and I feel a great weariness of this homeless life, and shrink from a repetition of stranger lands and scenes; but, as the cross and suffering connected with the route by England increases before my mind, so the conviction deepens that the Lord may require us to fulfil it.

Oct. 25.—This afternoon we took our accustomed walk outside the walls, and saw many ancient and scriptural way-marks. We passed out of the Damascus Gate, and followed the walls eastward, till we came to the upper valley of the Kidron above, and north of Gethsemane. A road leads through it, north-east, towards "Bethel." It is the loveliest vale in the circuit of the walls, and its picturesque, rock-terraced scenery, is here and there shaded by fig and olive trees. We passed a deep excavation in the side of the hill, which appeared like an ancient quarry; old trees are growing in its depth, and half-separated slabs remain a monument of other days. On the east side, the continuation of Olivet slopes away, and is lost among succeeding hills. A troop of Turks came scouring down the vale, with their Arab attendants, and their beautiful horses gaily caparisoned; they wore long robes of bright and varied colors, with rich turbans and glittering arms. As they passed they looked earnestly, with seeming surprise, at our unarmed simplicity, as few Europeans ride or walk so far without a guard. We followed the valley southward, on our return towards St. Stephen's Gate; and as it was still early, I sat down on a rock on the edge of the hill before it. Here the view is most beautiful and affecting, and I knew that I must soon leave these hallowed scenes. My health has been steadily improving since my sojourn in this country; I felt unusual strength, and watched with peculiar happiness the deepening shadows in the garden, while yet the golden rays of the setting sun lingered on the heights of Olivet! After I had finished a small sketch of Absalom's Pillar, that rose in the bottom of the vale, we returned, and sat late at tea with Meshullam and his family, listening to his eloquent recitals of joy and suffering, during his long residence in Palestine.

Oct. 26.—As our visit with Meshullam is drawing to a close, many questions of interest occupy our mutual attention, respecting the present transition state of this land, its greatest needs, and the most formidable obstacles in the way of its restoration. The most surprising fertility is struggling side by side with desert barrenness, and the choicest natural advantages, of climate and situation, have hitherto been paralyzed by an uncivilized despotism, and the ignorance and sloth of its occupants. But in the last few years a surprising change is distinctly manifest, and "*the land*," in harmony with the improving prospects of its scattered people, is showing symptoms of returning *life*, in sure presage of its speedy and glorious redemption. To show the confidence that his brethren repose in Meshullam I would mention, that two Rabbies have just left the room, who have been sitting with us an hour, consulting with him respecting some poor Jews, that have recently arrived, who each possess a little money; and these friends desire Meshullam's assistance in making some arrangement for their employment! We find difficulty in obtaining intelligence from Jaffa, and, unless some unexpected way shall soon open for our return by England, we must take the steamer next week from Jaffa to Beyroot, and thence proceed by the French line to Marseilles, where we can find vessels for America.

Oct. 27.—How mysterious are the ways of the Lord! and how often we recognise the inspired truth, "it is not in man to direct his steps!" The English Consul here was acquainted with our desire of obtaining a passage westward from Jaffa, but he left the city on a tour to Gaza, and we had no expectation of hearing from, or seeing him again. After he left, reasons unknown to us changed his plan, and he proceeded to Jaffa, where he found a merchant vessel belonging to England. He ascertained that the captain would accommodate us, and wrote and sent by his Arab express to inform us! We feel truly grateful for this kind attention; and as our convictions of duty coincide with this providential intimation, we have decided to leave immediately for Jaffa.

Oct. 28.—To-day, in the anxiety of preparation, I experienced a chill, and an attack of the fever, which at this season prevails within the walls, in consequence of the effluvia in the confined streets, arising from unremoved matter and destitution of sewers; also, just before the rainy season commences, the supply of water fails, or becomes low and poor in the old cisterns, and increases the tendency to disease; but I am happy to learn that in villages, where high walls do not obstruct the pure air, and there are wells and springs of living water, with common attention to health and cleanliness, no such tendency exists. The kind Christian lady who loaned me her saddle at Jaffa, having recently arrived in the city, called at the hotel to take leave of us. When she learned by what route we expect to return, a lady who accompanied her from England, and who came with her to-day, inquired if I had acquaintance or introduction there. She was surprised that we had not, and immediately offered me a letter to her sister residing there, if we visited her neighborhood, saying that she is a devoted Christian, and will take pleasure in affording us any needful advice or attention. She has since sent us a very kind introduction, and will also write by steamer, to anticipate us. When I consider the circumstances of humility under which I travel, such an unexpected and disinterested act of love, in this last moment of our need, much affects me, and I receive it as a new token of the Lord's goodness and approbation.

Oct. 29.—Our conversations have assumed the most serious and interesting character, and we feel united in one heart with our benevolent friend, in the spirit of entire self-sacrifice, to follow and carry out the purposes of God, in the openings of his divine providence, for the true good of Israel. He often regrets the shortness of our time; that we did not earlier and more freely communicate, and that we cannot visit with him different watered localities, where entire villages could soon be sustained by the fertility of the soil. Thousands of Israel are confined to the fœtid air of narrow dwellings, beneath these crumbling walls, without object or employment, rarely emerging beyond their sight, their weak animal existence scarcely sustained by a rigid charity, and dragging out a suffering existence, in all the horrors of destitution and ignorance; and this affliction is in their own land, where a small expenditure in agriculture, *connected with self-denying and active labors of love*, might at once liberate and introduce them into a position of hopeful blessing.

On one occasion he said, "This subject embraces the hope and interest of my whole *life!* I have sometimes spoken to distinguished men of piety, while they have been visiting this land, and they have encouraged me to hope in their co-operation; but when the sorrows of Jerusalem have faded from their sight, they have forgotten my poor appeal, and I have heard no more of their sympathy with Israel! Can it be that you also will forget? Why will you leave us? Remain at once, and unite with the humble means that we already have in possession, and prove what the Lord will do!" Such words of heart-felt earnestness and truth are sinking into our hearts, and if it were not that we esteem it a day of *good tidings*,—and that we owe a duty and "report" to the distant and beloved, who may also unite in the same holy service,—we should remain, and cast in our lot with a remnant of believing Israel, in the land of Judah! We have realized much spiritual life and blessing in our communications with this devoted man upon this subject; and if the Lord should spare our life, to testify to believers in our own land, and a few should be moved to come and colonize, without sectarian name or prejudice, with self-sacrifice to the one object, of obedience to God for the good of Israel, we will return and cheerfully unite with them, in so sweet and holy a service until the Master come.

Oct. 30.—My chills continue, and my kind friends, Mr. and Mrs. Meshullam, are much afflicted at my leaving them in this suffering state. Solomon has partially recovered, and is with us to-day. We cannot reconcile him to our departure, and his tears and entreaties increase my desire to return. He promises to join us, and learn agriculture, if we will come to the aid of Meshullam, and beseechingly holds up and counts his fingers for us to say how many moons before he may expect us! Our friend is much concerned to make the easiest arrangement for me, as I cannot take a comfortable seat in a carriage, or railway car, to pass the rough precipitous descent to Jaffa. The vessel is expected to sail on the 3d of November; and I cannot hope to recover in time, and must set out, while subject to chills and fever, on horseback, by the way.

Nov. 3.—On shipboard, at anchor before Jaffa. Every possible arrangement was made for our journey by Meshullam. He sent a muleteer and mules for our baggage, and Ahmud with necessary provisions. I was well wrapped, and seated in a pannier, suspended to the side of a strong mule, and Petro led the white donkey, ready saddled, to relieve me. Solomon came early, with a fixed purpose, notwithstanding his weakness, to lead my mule all the way to Jaffa. This we could not permit, but consented that he should walk a little distance on the road with us.—Meshullam also, with his youngest son in his arms, rode out some miles to attend us. Thus accompanied by these interesting friends—one a representative of Christian Israel, and the other of the sincere, but unbelieving of his brethren—early in the morning of the 1st of November, we left the Holy City. As I looked back, the sun had risen above the stony heights of Olivet, and surrounded by its olive shades, the grey walls of Jerusalem faded in the distance. My emotions were mingled with sorrow and joy—sorrow for the darkness and desolation that still enshrouds Zion, and joy at "the blessed hope" of her speedy redemption. At length we halted on a rocky summit, and covenanted, in the strength of the God of Israel, to give him no rest until he make Jerusalem a praise in the earth, and, according to his helping hand, to return in due time, and labor and abide with them. Our parting was painfully affecting, and poor Solomon was so weak, that Meshullam compelled him to take his saddle, while himself returned homeward on foot. At dark we reached Ramlah, found comfortable lodgings at the Latin Convent, and before noon the next day arrived at Jaffa. My chills were providentially stayed until evening, after which I experienced a severe attack, but to-day was enabled to come on board, expecting soon to lose sight of the land of prophetic promise.

March 30, 1850.—At sea, midway the Atlantic, on board an American steamer. Oh, what a mystery is human life! I little thought that five long months of suffering must intervene before I should write again. If possible, I would refrain from speaking a word of our fearful voyage of seventy-two days from Jaffa to England! I had severe chills and fever every day until Christmas, and we had a succession of head winds, rain, and terrible gales, keeping our berths wet or damp all the way. Our provisions were of the coarsest kind; and our captain proved to be one of the most unprincipled and severe of civilized humanity. I was reduced to the lowest state of existence; was unable to sit up an hour during the passage, and week after week despaired of life! But so it pleased the Lord to preserve me alive, until we landed in a storm, at Falmouth, England. Our provisions were nearly exhausted, (we had suffered much for want of food,) and our vessel and rigging rent and torn, having barely escaped shipwreck! The exertion and fatigue of landing brought on a violent relapse of fever, and my emaciation and helplessness was extreme.

Here we found that it was only a few hours, by steamer, to the place where our introduction was directed; if it had been otherwise, I could not have availed myself of its timely sympathy. We forwarded an intimation of our arrival, and on the fifth day I was carried on board the steamer. The distinguished lady, to whom we were directed, had received also a letter from Jerusalem respecting us, and received us with great kindness. She came with a carriage, and with Christian tenderness removed me to pleasant lodgings, which she had prepared for us — Here I hoped soon to regain strength, and proceed homewards; but the effects of my late disease and deprivation were fearful, and my broken frame seemed trembling for a long time between life and death. One relapse succeeded another, and one difficulty after another, would assume a formidable aspect, until two full months passed before I was able to take passage for the United States.

The Christian love, kind attention, and assistance which we received from a large circle of believers here, much affected my heart. I was most of the time confined to my room, and my spirit was so bruised and depressed, that at first I resolved to be silent respecting my heart's burden; but such was their sympathy, and the spiritual refreshment that we enjoyed in their communion, that we afterwards spoke freely to them of the character and position of Meshullam, and our interest in his sustainment. They were much pleased and quickened by the recital, and one of them, a gentleman of distinction, kindly proposed to take the charge and expense (through his agent in Liverpool) of any letters or freight which friends in America should wish to forward, through England, to the assistance of Meshullam. Here I saw why I had been sent to England, as there is no direct communication between the United States and Palestine! These were choice spirits, of great intelligence and scriptural knowledge, who also wait for the kingdom of God, and the consolation of Israel; and we parted from them with the most sincere emotions of love and gratitude.

April, 1850.—After this entry, we experienced an awful gale, which continued over a week. The wheels were often stopped, and many hours we were drifted by the fury of the winds and waves. The bulwarks and sky lights were swept away, and the water poured into the cabin, drenching the lower berths and loose baggage. The angry flood, unrestrained, broke over us, and our great ship rolled and plunged beneath their fearful weight, and seemed sinking to rise no more. Our captain, who had been at sea fifty years, remarked that he had never experienced so violent a storm; but such a scene must be witnessed, to feel its true power. Vain indeed was the wisdom, and mechanical skill of man in such an hour. Amid the consternation of all, we were enabled, through grace, to hope in God, that he would bring us up from this death also, and permit us to praise him for so great salvation! After long and suffering suspense the wind abated, and we reached our native land, overwhelmed with the sense of a Divine purpose of mercy in our preservation.

(Such was the interest of Christian friends in the cause of Meshullam, after our arrival, that I hastily collated a few written statements, which I had preserved respecting him, with extracts from this journal, (here omitted,) and published them early in June, 1850; which "narrative" is here (the FOURTH time) republished.)

NARRATIVE OF FACTS AND INCIDENTS

IN THE LIFE OF

JOHN MESHULLAM.

JOHN MESHULLAM was born in London, in the year 1800. His father was a wealthy and devout Jew, who purchased a vessel when his son was four years old, and embarked with his family for Jerusalem. On his way he stopped at Cadiz, where he heard of the embargo of Bonaparte, in the Mediterranean, which would interfere with the prosecution of his voyage; he therefore disposed of his vessel, and went by land to Salonica, where he settled, until the times should be more favorable to his pious design. John was sent back to a Jewish school at London, where he had only been a short time, when his father and mother, his brothers and sisters, were massacred, and their house pillaged and reduced to ashes, in an insurrection between the Turks and Greeks. As most of his father's money was secured in London, he became heir to a considerable estate. He continued at school, under the charge of the Jewish rabbies, until he was about fifteen years of age, when, in conjunction with an uncle, they attempted to coerce him to become one of their number, and cede his fortune to their common fund. He was opposed to this measure, and soon after left them, and proceeded to Berlin, where he pursued his studies, and became master of the German language.

When he was nineteen years of age, feeling a strong desire to visit Salonica, where his family had been massacred, he went and remained a short time with the Jews in that place While he was there, Joseph Wolff (whom he had never seen before) came into their synagogue, on the Sabbath, and began to address the Jews, on the subject of Messiah and his kingdom. This enraged them so much that they ejected him from the synagogue, and applied to the Pasha to take his life, and he was apprehended. Meshullam felt the most generous compassion for Wolff, and visited the Pasha, and interceded in his behalf. He advised him politely, to take heed as to his decision respecting him, that he was of another and higher class of the Jews, who only wished to reform some of their superstitious errors, and moreover was an *English* subject. The Pasha thanked him for this information, and released Mr. W. But the Jews were so incensed against him that his life was still in danger. Perceiving this, he sent his servant to procure horses, and himself escorted him by night beyond their reach.

Meshullam was still a firm believer in the faith of his fathers, and soon after proceeded to Jerusalem, where he remained three years. He acquired the Arabic language, and with great difficulty searched out the land, and became familiar with each dear locality mentioned in the Scriptures. This required great courage, energy, and endurance, as the state of the country was then much more fearful than at present. He desired to fulfil his father's original design, but felt a peculiar restlessness of spirit, without a purpose or a home, and resolved to extend his travels. He visited the Levant, Turkey, Persia, the East Indies, Arabia, Egypt, Palestine and Jerusalem the second time, France, Germany, Prussia, Austria, Russia, Sweden, Norway, Great Britain, the United States, North and South America, and the West Indies. Wherever he went he sought to acquire the language, and now speaks thirteen fluently. He finally returned to London, and soon after accidentally heard that Joseph Wolff was to preach in a certain chapel. Though he had never visited a place of Christian worship he felt a curious desire to see Mr. W., and accordingly went to hear him. Soon after he entered, Mr. W. espied him, and exclaimed to the audience: "There is the young man who saved my life, of whom I have told you," and compelled him to come forward and take a seat near him. After listening to an animated discourse on the subject of the coming of Christ and his kingdom, M. retired with mingled sensations; and the inquiry was then first started in his mind, "Can it be that JESUS of Nazareth is the Messiah of our Scriptures?" This conviction followed him, and afterwards, wherever he went, he sought every secret opportunity to hear Christ preached.

On leaving London he went to Italy, and at Genoa he married the eldest daughter of a Jewish banker of wealth and influence. There he commenced business operations, which he prosecuted with success, and was much esteemed by his father-in-law and the Jews generally. His two eldest sons, Elijah and James, were born at Genoa. As he was retiring from Christian service at the English Consul's, one day a Jew discovered him, and persecution immediately followed. His father-in-law was frantic, and closely interrogated him. M could not deny his convictions, although he had never communicated with Christians, and was scarcely established in the faith of Jesus. Such was the excitement that soon prevailed against him, that he was obliged suddenly to break up his establishment, at a great pecuniary loss, and flee to Leghorn, where he again commenced business, was prosperous, and secretly heard the preached *word*. After a time, however, his father-in-law pursued him, in order to take from him his wife and sons. Not being able to persuade or coerce his daughter, he exposed M's apostacy to the Jews in Leghorn. Persecutions, more bitter than he had hitherto encountered, now obliged him, though in the winter season, to leave Leghorn at a great sacrifice of his property. He then sought a refuge in Tunis; but on his arrival there he was unable to procure either a house or rooms for his accommodation. After making every effort he finally obtained an open OUT-HOUSE of an English resident. This afforded little protection from the rain; but after covering the roof with coarse oil-cloth, he placed therein his dear wife, in feeble health, and his little ones, together with his merchandise and baggage. Their situation was so uncomfortable that he soon projected building a house. The season was unpropitious, and there were no boards, timber, or stone, to be obtained in the city. In the absence of these he contrived a mixture of pebbles and mud, which he moulded with his packing boxes, and secured a roof with bamboos, covered with heavy oil-cloth, of which he providentially had a supply. He thus, in a short time, secured a residence for his family. Though his means had become greatly reduced by the sudden breaking up and sacrifice of his two former establishments, he again began to succeed in mercantile pursuits.

About this time he became fearful of Jewish influence upon his sons, and hearing of a Christian missionary (F. M. Ewald,) who was about returning to England, he applied to him to take charge of them, and place them in a Christian school in London. Mr. Ewald was surprised, and exclaimed, "But you are a Jew; how can this be?" Mr. Meshullam answered, "Though I am esteemed such, I desire my sons to be Christians." This was his first confession to a Christian. After his children were gone, the Jews in Tunis understood his position, and the fire of persecution again kindled around him to such an extent that he was obliged to leave suddenly, and removed to Malta, where he hoped to enjoy the protection of the British government. So great had been this last sacrifice cf property that he was unable longer to follow his former business. In his early travels, several merchants had sent by him, to different places, for rare dye-stuffs, and several valuable receipts had thus come into his possession. In his present extremity he improved this knowledge by setting up a dyeing establishment, which was surprisingly patronised, not only at Malta, but also by merchants and manufacturers in different ports in the Mediterranean, and he succeeded in a great variety of the choicest colors.

At Malta he became acquainted with Mr. Gobat, the present Bishop of Jerusalem, who had not then received orders in the church. They became much attached to each other, and Meshullam insisted on his baptizing himself and wife, who sympathized with him in the hope of the Gospel of Christ. Mr. Gobat hesitated on account of his want of authority, but at length yielded to his desire. After some time his new occupation so seriously affected his health that he was obliged to relinquish it; after which he resolved to leave Malta, and settle finally in Jerusalem. Mr. Gobat and his English friends proposed his accepting a situation in connection with the Mission at that place, which would afford him a comfortable living. This he steadily declined, saying that he could not conscientiously eat the bread that might be given to a more worthy agent, so essential in such a holy cause, and that he would cast himself wholly on the Lord, whose kind providence had so long supported him.

On his arrival at Jerusalem he found the city destitute of almost every comfort and convenience requisite to an European family. He received, about this time, a small legacy inherited by the will of his wife's father, (a mere pittance to that which she should have received,) and conceived the idea of furnishing the European residents with the necessaries of life. He imported furniture, groceries, and merchandise, of various kinds, from Malta, England, etc. For some time he succeeded so well, that he finally sent to London for a large and choice supply, in which he invested most of his capital. This expensive cargo arrived safely in Beyroot. His agent there put them on board of two open Arab craft, without any responsible person to take charge of them, and, with the exception of two barrels of potatoes, they were all lost in the surf near Jaffa. He soon received the intelligence, and hastened to Jaffa to learn the circumstances of his loss. He returned with the potatoes to his family; but a hot fever was raging in his veins, which prostrated him for a long time, with little hope of life. Meanwhile a person having a small claim against him, seized upon and took possession of his store, and sold out its choice effects at an entire sacrific which, with other expenses and extortions during his long illness, completed his ruin, and left him without bread. His wife endeavored to console him, and assured him that God was still the same, and would surely provide. One barrel of the potatoes was opened, on which for some time they principally subsisted. There was a small piece of waste soil connected with M's residence, which, as his strength slowly revived, he determined to plant with the remaining potatoes. This was a *mere experiment*, as no vegetables had succeeded in the city, and potatoes were unknown in Palestine. A large sum had been yearly appropriated to the Mission for the support of a garden for the benefit of their hospital, and although they had, with the assistance of skilful gardeners, made every effort, they had entirely failed. When he began he was so weak that he was often obliged to sit down. His third son, Peter, a small lad, said: "Father, I will help you;" and really assisted him much, until the whole plat was slowly planted.

While these were growing, the season of the pilgrims (Easter) filled the city to overflowing with visiters. An English nobleman arrived with his family, and was unable to procure lodgings for them. In his extremity he was directed to M., who, since his arrival at Jerusalem, has ever been of great service to the European residents, the Missions, and travellers generally, on account of his correct knowledge of the place, and the different languages spoken there. This gentleman sought his assistance; and M. generously offered him his whole house, and removed his family into a small, uncomfortable room, adjoining, assisted him in all his arrangements for visiting different and distant localities, and in his consequent intercourse with the Arabs. This was so appreciated by the gentleman that he paid him liberally, and encouraged him to hire a larger house, and open it for the accommodation of European travellers. He left him all his travelling furniture, and sent him more from Beyroot on his way home, as furniture is extremely expensive and difficult to be obtained in Jerusalem. This was the commencement of his hotel, which he has gradually improved. He has kept it for several years with great success, and the approbation of all.

But to return to his experiment in cultivation, to which such repeated and strange providences had driven him.

To the astonishment of his neighbors, his potatoes grew and yielded a most abundant crop, from which, after using for his family, and reserving for seed, he realized the sum of fifty guineas!! He felt as if *God had spoken*, and received his success as directly from his hand. Meshullam believes in the personal coming and reign of Christ, and his kingdom at hand. He is waiting and watching the fulfilment of the Prophetic Scriptures, in reference to the return of a remnant of his brethren, the justification of the sanctuary, and the restoration of the land. He then began to reflect more seriously on this token of the Lord's willingness to bless the cultivation of the soil, which has been so long desolate. As he was riding one day in the vicinity of *Bethlehem*, near the Pools of Solomon, he discovered a rich valley, in an uncultivated state, with the different kinds of native fruit, the fig, pomegranate, and vine, growing untrained. It was also watered by a large and living fountain. On inquiry he ascertained that the owners, having murdered their neighbors some years before, and being unable to pay the price of blood, according to the Turkish law, had fled the country. M. went to the Pasha, and paid the stipulated sum; he sent for the banished to return, and gave them half the soil, and entered into a continuous lease for the remainder, paying them a small sum yearly. This is the only way in which Europeans can legally obtain possession of the soil. He provided them seed for their part, and employs them as laborers on his own, and has thus become their benefactor, and secured their confidence. This was in 1845, since which time he constantly acknowledges the hand of God in his *unprecedented* success. He now raises *five* crops in a *year!** of different kinds of European vegetables,

* As some have been surprised at the statement that the soil is capable of producing FIVE crops of vegetables in a year, I here insert the copy of a little memorandum, which I wrote at the time, from Mr. Meshullam's lips, as to the alternations and kinds of vegetables, and the months producing them.

He said, "with irrigation I can raise five crops of vegetables in a year." I then asked him to repeat their names, order and time, and most of which were unknown in Judea before. He raises two crops without irrigation, during the wet season, and three during the dry, through the plentiful supply of water from the fountain. His first crop he dedicated to the Lord, and distributed it among the poor Jews, although he might have realized a large sum by its disposal in the city. He has also obtained by lease, a vineyard and several fields of wheat and grain, about three-quarters of a mile distant, in the valley above the Pools.

In "Solomon's Castle," a few rods distant from the Pools, he finds shelter for his laborers and cattle, the inside area being large enough for them all, the outside walls still remaining entire. He has great difficulty in obtaining seeds, and any field, fruit, or garden seeds that would be useful for food, would be of exceeding value to him. The destitution of vegetables, and the abject poverty of many of the most devout Jews, speak the urgency of this need. He has just received liberty from the Pasha to build a small house in "Artos," (the name which the Arabs give to the Valley of Bethlehem,) and has resolved to dispose of his hotel and remove thither with his family trusting alone in God, to protect him from the wild Arabs, and the many jealousies opposing his course among professing religious sects in Jerusalem. We will only add a few of many *incidents* that came to our knowledge, while residing intimately two months in his interesting family, last autumn:—

1. After the first crop of potatoes in his garden, in the city, he began to clear the soil of its many stones, and for this purpose commenced digging a deep pit in the midst, in which to deposit them; but he had only dug a few feet before his servant, by a heavy stroke, broke into a covered arch, in which, to his joy and surprise, he discovered a deep reservoir of water. This afterwards proved

he replied: "In October, I plant potatoes; in January, carrots or beets; in April, potatoes again; in July I get beans in 28 days. Also, another crop of beans in August.

Without water, I can raise two crops yearly. In April, I plant cauliflowers and cabbage; or in December, wheat, barley, oats, or potatoes."

to be an unfailing fountain, from which, in times of drought in the dry season, he has sold to the Pasha and his soldiery, and the Turks, (as water is sold in the city at such times,) but he gave it freely to his poor brethren, the Jews, besides watering his garden abundantly, giving drink to his horses and donkeys, and other family uses. This blessing *he receives* as peculiarly from the Lord.

2. When he arrived in Jerusalem in 1840, it was very difficult to obtain good bread, and European residents and travellers suffered much on this account. The wheat is poorly cleaned from the ground threshing, and is ground between two rude stones, as in ancient times. This is done principally by WOMEN; the flour is coarse, and, being destitute of suitable bolting-sieves, the bran is only partially separated. Meshullam had brought with him fine sieves and bolting-cloths from Malta. With the help of an Arab he built a stone oven with his own hands, and thus furnished good bread for his family. The wife of a missionary, who was in the habit of visiting them, was much pleased with their bread, and entreated, as a favor, that he would supply her with a loaf daily. Other families soon interceded in like manner, and were also supplied; but the demand increasing beyond his means, he conceived the idea of setting up a bake-house, to employ two of his destitute brethren, as there is no work they can get in Jerusalem. With great difficulty he taught two of them, and built them an oven, advanced money to buy wheat, and continued, with strange patience, to assist them, till they now obtain a good living, and supply the city with excellent bread. A great contrast to the previous destitution.

3. Meshullam having need of much wheat for his establishment, the Arabs were in the habit of bringing it to him from distant villages. In the year 1843 they brought an unusual supply. He refused none that came, until he had a large room entirely filled, and his wife feared he should never dispose of it. Just at this time a singular phenomenon appeared in the sky, (the reputed comet, regarding which there were so many speculations in Europe and America at that time;) this so much alarmed the in-

habitants of Palestine, that they decided that a great famine was near. The price of wheat began accordingly to rise, and such was the panic that M. was entreated by many to sell his store. The Pasha offered five times its first cost, but he refused. The English families wanted it also, but he still retained it, until the distress became dreadful among the poor Jews. M. then sent them word to come, and sold to each of them *one measure* of wheat at the low wholesale price which he gave for it, until all was exhaused, reserving only a few measures for himself. He lost much, as he gave them good measure, and had received scant measure from the Arabs. Soon after, by the time *the measure* was consumed among the poor, the panic ceased, and wheat was plentiful.

4. At another time, when the rain set in so early, that it prevented the mountain Arabs from bringing into the city the usual supply of charcoal for the winter, it occasioned great suffering. The Pasha had every camel load that came to the gates seized for his establishment and soldiery. In this extremity Meshullam rode out to the mountains, and bought twenty camel loads of charcoal, and came with them to the gates. The guard demanded it, but M. refused, and went to the Pasha, who still insisted on having it. M. said: "You have encouraged me to keep a house for travellers, and I must have this charcoal to cook their food." The Pasha yielded, and M. secured it, and afterwards divided all he could spare among his poor brethren. He advanced several a little money, and told them to go outside with donkeys, and buy charcoal in small quantities, and retail it in the city, and thus a number still obtain their living.

5. An Arab Sheik, who resided in the vicinity of Meshullam's farm, was moved with great envy as he watched his success, and seemed inclined to do him all the injury in his power. The seed wheat of M. is much superior to that of the Arabs, having taken great pains to clean it from the wild seeds that are often mixed with it. One season this Shiek was destitute of seed, and applied to M. to supply him, to which M. readily consented, requiring a smaller

share of the crop than the law of the Pasha allows in such cases. The Sheik's crop was unusually abundant that year, but when he came to return to M. the stipulated measure, he found it nearly half composed of dirt and small pebbles, so that it was worth very little to him. Mrs. M. remonstrated with the Sheik, and told him that they had given choice wheat and good measure, and that such conduct was unjust in the sight of God, and he could not prosper in such a course. In a week after 119 of his flock of sheep strangely sickened, and died. Some of the friendly Arabs told him that it was on account of his dishonesty to M. He still, however, continued his opposition. Soon after this, his wife suddenly died; he married again, and this wife in a short time became blind. M. obtained leave from the Pasha to build a house at Artos, and went with some masons to commence. The Sheik thought he had M. now in his power (as the Turkish law prohibits any European building;) he saddled his favorite donkey, and rode over with his attendants to forbid him. He left his donkey to feed at a little distance on the side of the hill, and while he was angrily denouncing M. and rejecting every explanation, one of his servants came running to tell him that his donkey had fallen down among the rocks, and broken his neck; a most singular occurrence! Some present remarked that it was because of his persecutions of M. He retired greatly chagrined. Undeterred, however, in his malicious purpose, he went to Jerusalem to enter suit against him. In opening his case the Pasha inquired: "Why do you oppose this man? has he injured our country? has he pulled down or destroyed anything? Has he not, ever since he came among us, been a benefit to our people, by his industry and constant efforts to build up? *Let him build;* and if I hear of any further opposition from yourself or others, it will be followed by severe punishment." The Sheik was overawed, and will dare no longer to afflict M.

6 Another Arab neighbor, with the same feelings of enmity, sought in every secret way to injure him. Three times Meshullam discovered him making depredations on

his farm, and reproved, and then forgave him. At length, gaining confidence in his clemency, the Arab made a gap in M.'s wall, and let in his goats and sheep, to the great injury of some of his choicest plants. M. thought he would then appeal to the Pasha, that he might be more thoroughly reproved. After the Pasha had heard the testimony of M.'s Arab laborers, he was highly incensed against the offender, and determined to fine him a large sum. To this M. strongly objected, saying that he was willing to forgive him this fourth time, if he would promise not to trespass again. The Pasha then insisted that he should pay the whole amount of damages. M. would not permit this, but said that he wanted no money, but only peace. The Pasha then became vexed at M. and ordered the man to prison. M. remained in the court a short time, talking with the Pasha, and then so earnestly entreated that the prisoner should be released, that he complied. The prison was again unlocked, and the Arab was brought into their presence. The Pasha reprimanded him severely, assuring him that through the intercession of M. he was liberated, but threatened him that he would surely fine him heavily for all preceding offences, and imprison him beside, if he heard of any repetition of annoyance to M.; adding, that he was ashamed of him as a Mussulman, standing in such dark contrast with this Christian! who had so often forgiven him.

7. At the return of the locusts, one year, they were unusually numerous and destructive. They literally darkened the air, and wherever they settled they consumed every green thing. This season Meshullam's garden in the city, and his fields at Artos, were unusually promising, and he trembled before the Lord as to the result. Their approach drew near, and, although he had never heard of a remedy, he conceived the idea of making a great smoke in his garden. Having no wood, he took old clothes and rags as a substitute, and made a fire in the centre. He then left it, and rode out of the city to see the fate of Artos, which he found unscathed, the locusts having flown over that deep valley and settled on many Arab fields on the hills adjacent, entirely destroying them. He returned to

the city, the black cloud hovering there, and found that the smoke had been successful; his garden was spared, and the locusts had fallen a foot deep in many places near.—This great deliverance he attributes entirely to the interference of the Lord.

8. His love and endurance towards his poor and unbelieving brethren is very great. It is his habit to distribute loads of vegetables and greens among them, in their times of greatest need; and they often come to him for advice and assistance. He has been the means of opening several ways by which many individuals have obtained a support, and a number of intelligent converts were first moved by his ACTS of love to confess to him their convictions, and listen to his earnest entreaties. to embrace the truth, and are now hopeful Christians.

9. A pious gentleman from England, *en route* for India, put up at Meshullam's hotel some weeks. He had two Jewish servants with him, who went with him to India.—After a long time these Jews returned, with a letter from the gentleman desiring M. to receive them into his house, and keep them until he should hear from him again. He stated that his reasons for such a request was the state of their minds, which he supposed to be much exercised on the subject of Christianity. M. received them kindly, gave them a room, and fed them at his own table. They remained, going out and coming in, eating and drinking, not offering to assist M. in his many duties, neither showing the least concern for their salvation. They drank much wine, and found fault with their food. At length M. heard that they had obtained money for dissipations through credit of being with him! He was much tried to know his duty, fearing to quench the last hope of their conversion, and having great pity for them. When they first came they professed a desire to go to Damascus, so he conceived the plan of fulfilling it, after they had remained with him about a year. He hired horses and a guide, supplied them with provisions, and had some difficulty in getting them peaceably away. After they were gone he went round the city and ascertained that they had accumulated a great

debt in his name. Every poor person that had sold them clothing, shoes, and other necessaries, he repaid; but their bills for wine, spirits, etc., he declined. He never heard from the gentleman.

10. Upon one occasion, when he had need of a head waiter, an Italian applied for the situation, professing great experience. Meshullam asked him what religion he professed; he answered, "the Roman Catholic." M. then told him to repeat the Lord's Prayer; but he could not.—M. looked anxiously in his face and said, "You are a Jew; oh, never be ashamed to own your people!" The man then confessed that he was an Israelite, and entered into service with him. The first day showed that he knew nothing about serving tables. M. then tried him in different positions in his hotel, but found him incapable in all. He sent him to his private house, a few steps distant, to see if Mrs. M. could do anything with him. She ascertained that he had once learned the tailor's trade. She procured cloth, had it cut out, and set him about making some clothes for himself, as he was most destitute. This occupied him a long time; after which he showed no disposition to be useful in any way, and manifested a want of all religion. After keeping him through the fall and winter, M. strove to rouse his energies to seek some employment, to which he showed great reluctance. M. then raised him a purse of about five pounds from his visiters, M. adding one pound unknown to Mrs. M., while she at the same time gave another, without his knowledge. Still the poor little man would not go, saying, "What can I do with this money?" and pushed it from him. M. at last persuaded him, took horses, and went himself with him to Jaffa, obtained lodgings and employment with a tailor for him, and returned home with a happy conscience.

11. A gentleman arrived at his hotel from Egypt by the way of the desert, with the usual attendants, a dragoman, (which is the name for an interpreter and agent,) and several muleteers. After the baggage was conveyed to his room, the gentleman missed a carpet bag, containing three hundred pounds. He immediately called Meshullam and informed

10

him of his loss, and said, "It must be the dragoman, who is a young Jew, whom I found in Alexandria." This grieved M., and he responded: "Have you any reason for this suspicion?" The gentleman could give none. M. then offered to take the affair into his own hands. He went out and questioned the Jew, whom he found to be an interesting youth, who solemnly asserted his innocence. He sought and interrogated the muleteers; being dissatisfied with their answers, he took them before the Pasha. After some examination, the whip was applied to one who seemed the most confused, who, after a few strokes, confessed that he had secreted it in a village, a few miles back; from whence M. sent and recovered it. M. took the bag to the gentleman, and seriously reproved him for so carelessly injuring the reputation of one who had no other support. He then took the youth aside, and asked him why he had chosen an occupation so liable to disrepute. The young man replied that he had no other resource M. perceiving that he was intelligent, and feeling a great pity for him, said "If you will leave this service, you are welcome to remain with me until the Lord shall provide some better way." This kind offer the youth gladly accepted. He engaged with M. at liberal wages, and remained some time in his employ. His mind became interested and awakened, and he received the faith of Jesus Christ. M. perceiving that he possessed considerable talent, was successful in interesting several friends in England in his behalf, who sent for him and placed him at school and then at college, where he well improved his opportunities. He is now a travelling missionary among his brethren in the East.

12. While Meshullam resided in Tunis, a Jew was unjustly cast into prison, with no hope of liberation, as he had no friend to be security for him. M. accidentally heard of it, and though he must hazard much, he determined to procure his release, as the confinement was such as to endanger life. With considerable difficulty he effected it, and the Jew for a time seemed very grateful. He often visited M., and at length became attached to Mrs. M.'s female domestic, whom they had brought with them there. They

were married, commenced housekeeping, and had two children. Meanwhile the Jew occupied himself in pawnbroking, and dealt with great injustice and extortion. For this, Mr. and Mrs. M. often faithfully reproved him. The more hardened the Jew became in this course, the more strict and legal he was in every outward observance of the Jewish ritual, which greatly surprised M. One night, when he was absent from home, some of the inhabitants who had been defrauded, broke into the house of the Jew, and murdered his wife and children. In the greatest agony of soul, he came to tell M., and when Mrs. M. strove to improve the opportunity to persuade him to alter his ways, supposing his afflictions had come in judgment upon him, he cried out "Oh, no, no; not for that alone; but it is because I have read the New Testament, and have been convinced that Jesus is our Messiah, and yet have not *confessed* him!!" After deep repentance he obtained forgiveness, and, by an humble and consistent life afterward, proved his sincere faith in our Lord Jesus Christ, which was more and more confirmed by the *love*, and testimony of M.

13. Another poor Jew, in Jerusalem, was living near the house of a rich Mussulman, who sought every opportunity to beat and oppress him. One day Meshullam happened to pass by, and witnessed the sufferings of his poor brother. He immediately interfered, and asked, "Why do you abuse this poor man? What evil hath he done?" And added, that he would complain to the Pasha, if he should repeat such conduct. The Jew, with the greatest earnestness, entreated M. to desist, saying, "I am a poor Jew, and the time of our deliverance is not yet come; God is angry with us, and I would *patiently* suffer all His righteous displeasure." M. told me this to illustrate the faith and humility of some of the poor.

14. Some few years since, when the English Mission were about erecting their church on Mount Zion, they were obliged to remove some forty feet of debris, or rubbish, so as to place the foundations sure upon the rock. To do this, they must need many common laborers. Meshullam

applied to them to employ the poor Jews, who were in such perishing need. Many had reported and believed the scandal, that the Jews in Jerusalem would not do servile labor, even if they had employment, which report has closed the hearts of many professing Christians against them. This objection was now made, but M. insisted on the experiment. After some hesitation, they were employed, and to the surprise of every one, several hundred more than were needed offered themselves for a small pittance per day.—Meshullam was, however, finally disappointed in his kind design, for they could not work on the Sabbath, (the Seventh day) neither on their feast days. So the architect, after using them awhile, dismissed them, and employed the Arabs. This case is only mentioned to refute the common idea of the indolence of the Jews.

15. A gentleman from Europe, who is an Israelite of great wealth, and feels a kind regard for the state of the poor Jews in Jerusalem, visited them last summer and contributed largely toward their relief. He had numerous travelling attendants, and one, a Christian gentleman of some distinction, lodged at Meshullam's hotel. It seemed to be the object of his benevolent patron, if possible, to commence some establishment, or make an arrangement for the employment and support of the distressed poor among his people. In looking round in vain for a capable and proper agent, and some plan of relief, that such an agent with his means, would carry out with success, his discerning mind could only see *Meshullam!* whose constant kindness and aid to the Jews had reached his notice. He, therefore, sent proposals to M. by this *Christian*, that if he would return to the faith of his fathers and take charge of the work, he would make him a fortune, and he who promised, was abundantly able to perform. M. calmly replied: "Tell Sir —— that I have made my fortune by confessing *Jesus Christ.*

These are only a few of many incidents of the same character, which came to my knowledge while residing with him at Bethlehem and at Jerusalem. Upon one occasion some English travellers obtained for him the appointment of Consul at Jaffa, which he declined At another time he was offered a considerable salary, in connection with the Mission as general interpreter; but he still chooses to labor on in this humble way, and trust alone in God.

It is surprising that such self-sacrificing efforts should excite any but the kindest feelings in the hearts of professing Christians in his vicinity; but, instead of sympathy and aid, he is the object of envy and cruel prejudice, and seems struggling alone in this path of duty and sacrifice. To illustrate this, I would add, that the week before we left, a delegation from one of the convents (not Roman Catholic) offered the Pasha 7,000 piastres to stop Meshullam's cultivation in Artos!

We have been constrained by the love of Christ to give this relation of what we have seen and heard, being fully convinced that the Lord has been, *in a peculiar manner*, sustaining this true Israelite. He is the first Christian Hebrew who has succeeded in cultivating the soil of his fathers since the dispersion. Through his *sustainment* and blessing we believe that God has a design of opening an humble way of escape and salvation to a "*remnant*" of his ancient people. This cannot be effected by direct preaching or other spiritual effort; but if Meshullam had means supplied to extend his farming operations, he would give his starving brethren employment, and hundreds would gladly offer themselves to labor with him at two and a half piastres per day (the same as five and a half pence, or eleven cents,) which would bring them under the influence of his Christ-like love and example. It would make them independent of the charity fund of the Rabbies, to which they are now in bondage, and which is scarcely sufficient to sustain life in the coarsest and most frugal manner. Those who are already inquiring, and half convinced of the truth among the pious poor, would have a refuge, and be placed in a position where they might afterwards be reached and won by the love of Christ.

It must be distinctly understood that Meshullam makes

no appeal for himself, and will receive nothing; for the Lord has so prospered him in his recent course, that he is helping others; but he is willing, *without reward*, to apply any assistance that the friends of Christ may send to relieve his poor brethren and win them to the truth, for the preparation of "a remnant," to meet the Lord at his coming.

On returning I mentioned his case to a circle of believers in England, who have become interested for him, and will contribute something to hold up his hands in this laborious, disinterested work of the Lord. Many Christians profess great sympathy for the Jews, and are waiting, I humbly trust, for "the set time" to favor Zion, when God will surely open their way to show the sincerity and efficiency of their *love*. If there are any who deserve their sympathy and aid, it must be the devoted and suffering poor in Jerusalem. Here is a simple door which providence alone has unsealed and opened to such, by which the charities of sincere and willing hearts may be sent to them, and most judiciously applied by one of their own brethren.

Whatever time, suffering, and sacrifice this humble report has cost the writer, is *freely given*, in the most perfect confidence that the same love which commenced this work in Meshullam's hands will succeed, and bring it to a blessed accomplishment. If any thing beyond its expense is realized from the sale of this work, it will be faithfully appropriated to the same object. I will add here the testimony of disinterested men and Christians, as to the general character of M. Also, the testimony of one who has known him for many years, an intimate friend to whom M. is much attached, who says, "I am sure he will make the best use of it,"—which together with his own untiring example of self-sacrifice to the same object, is sufficient to satisfy the *willing* mind that this is no common appeal, but a "CRY" from Jerusalem—"Come over and help us."

THE TESTIMONY OF TRAVELLERS.

The following we copied from his dining-room album, which contained many other testimonials:

MR. EDWARD WILLING, } Philadelphia, U. S. America.
MR. T. LINDSAY GILLESPIE, }

From Cairo *en route* to Damascus.)

March 10th, 1849.

After a five days' residence at Mr. Meshullam's house, we have great pleasure in expressing our satisfaction with the attention which we have received.

June 6th, 1849.

I shall not, I trust, soon forget how much I am indebted to you for arrangements with dragomen, muleteers, Arabs, and all the necessary evils of this country, when your disinterested judgment did what I could not manage for myself.

WM. JAMES WOODCOCK.

JERUSALEM, November 14th, 1848.

The Rev. F. N. Allen, Chaplain in the Honorable East India Company's Service, and Mrs. Allen, spent nearly a month in Mr. M.'s hotel, during the first of which they were much indebted to him and Mrs. Meshullam for their attentions during severe illness. They found the hotel the cleanest and most comfortable they have met during a tour in Egypt and Syria, and derived great advantage from the assistance of Mr. Meshullam in all their transactions with the natives of the country, and in preparations of their journey through the desert to Cairo. F. N. ALLEN.

JERUSALEM, Hotel Book, October 23d, 1848.

All the officers of the United States Expedition to the Dead Sea have at different times lodged in this house, and are unanimous in the expression of their entire satisfaction in every respect; independent of the faithful performance of the duties of a host, Mr. Meshullam has been exceedingly friendly and serviceable.

(Signed) W. F. LYNCH, *Commander*.

The following testimony is from the gentleman who took the charge of his two sons from Tunis to London:

JERUSALEM, October 29th, 1849.

I have great pleasure in testifying, that I have known Mr. Meshullam and his family since the year 1835; that they were brought to the knowledge of Christ Jesus, and that they were subsequently baptized at Malta, 1840, by the present Bishop of Jerusalem. Mr. M. and his family settled in the Holy City in 1840, and has endeavored to maintain himself and family by his own industry. A short time ago he turned his attention to agriculture, and is now cultivating the ground, in which he has so well succeeded, that he has resolved to devote himself entirely to that occupation, and to give up his hotel, which he has kept for several years in Jerusalem. Any assistance which Christian friends might grant him, IN HIS LAUDABLE UNDERTAKING, is well bestowed, and I am sure he will make the best use of it.

F. M. EWALD, *Chaplain to the Right Reverend the Lord Bishop of the Anglican Church at Jerusalem, and Missionary to the Jews in the Holy City.*

LETTERS.

ELIJAH, the eldest son of Meshullam, is attached to his father, and seems truly to appreciate his position, and the efforts he is making for the good of Israel. Just before we left, he gave me a paper containing some of his own thoughts respecting the good to be obtained by introducing industrial occupation in agriculture among the Jews. He is a young man of promise and conscientious uprightness, and his constant use of the Arabic language in speaking and writing, will account for the difficulty of his English style. The following is an extract from his testimony:

"*Honorable Friends:*—These few lines, however imperfect their language may be, are chiefly designed to encourage those benevolent friends who, from hearty sympathy, seek the temporal and spiritual welfare of the long-desolated Zion. That through your aid the now (for centuries) alienated children of Abraham may be roused, and encouraged to labor as the above-named Israelite, my father, has done in the vineyards of our fathers. Most particularly now the change of events fully testify their approaching restoration to this land. For eighteen centuries their longing desire and eyes have been fixed upon it, and its ancient possessors are yet no more than strangers and miserable captives. The simplest manner, conducive to this end, would give greater success to those several communities who spend their exertions and means for the support of their proselytes, if they would encourage the Jews, by the same expenditure, to cultivate and rebuild their father-land. This would commence a work worthy to be appreciated and extended, by all those friends concerned for their eternal welfare. What should inspire us more for their restoration than their pious zeal, which constantly bedews with their tears the soil around the broken fragments of their Temple—the soil which so many thousands of their forefathers have watered by their blood? The success of agriculture has been so advanced by these efforts, that five crops [of different grains and vegetables] can be yearly gathered with the greatest certainty, so that we can only trust that many may be aided to follow my father's example, and with him share the happy results. This will soon bring many of the desolate families of the Jews, who now live in subterranean vaults and caves, to seek this succor for their temporal relief. It is our fervent desire that this enterprise may be extended for that people, who, though afflicted for their disobedience, are still beloved by the Almighty, who knows that we also are liable to the same, notwithstanding our holiest exertions to be meet partakers and guests in the heavenly Jerusalem, the throne of the Everlasting God and our Redeemer Jesus Christ. With all your interest for this labor, and your liberality for its promotion, never forget to pray for the peace of Jerusalem, that the following Scripture may be yours: 'They shall prosper that love thee.' "

"ELIJAH MESHULLAM."

Since this narrative was first published, we have received two letters from Meshullam; the last contains the interesting intelligence, that he has indeed removed from his successful hotel in Jerusalem, to the solitary valley of Artos, near Bethlehem, and embarked his entire energies and interest in this arduous labor of benevolence. We here subjoin extracts of each letter, but his long disuse of English composition, represents him with great injustice:

JERUSALEM, March 20th, 1850.

"*My Dear Christian Friends*:—I cannot but express an unreserved gratitude at the acknowledgment of your kind letter, which reached me on the 17th inst., as we felt much concern at the state in which you left Jerusalem. But we could not realize, that we should be the objects of such sympathy and interest, in an epoch when the true friends of Israel are so amazingly scarce. Such disinterestedness cannot but be highly gratifying, upon due consideration of the eminent good which might, with assured success, be performed to this once prosperous land, were our energetic labours to meet with equal approbation from a few such friends as you profess sincerely to be towards us." * * * * * * "in justice to myself, I must not omit mentioning the bishop of Jerusalem, as a conjoined friend, who, like you, anxiously seeks the promotion of my enterprise. It is, however, evident that some deleterious stupor is blinding the minds of others, who, partially informed of my intentions, do not appreciate the benefit so clearly to be derived from you, by such an introduction of industrious labor —as my affairs in Artos have hitherto been extended with more than apparent success. I trust you will not think me presuming, if I herein mention my anxiety of enlarging this work, and my son, Elijah, promises to forward to you the general accounts I shall have to give about Artos, every favorable opportunity. Allow me to express my thankfulness for the seeds which I received, inclosed in your letter, [some *cabbage seeds*, which I cemented with gum Arabic, to the inside of our first letter from England,] and, above all, for the mill you propose to commission through England for me. As to Solomon, Elijah, since your departure, has tried every possible way to relieve him, and the Doctor has administered those remedies which have restored him to perfect health; and in the meantime, I am trying with all my mind, to remedy his circumstances, and I will not fail to distribute discreetly, and according to necessity, any offerings that Christian friends will be led to make." * * * * * * * "Permit me to conclude with the conjoined regards of myself and family, praying fervently that the entrusted love you have towards us, may meet its due reward in the heavenly Jerusalem of peace. Meanwhile, I shall not omit praying for all those friends who are engaged and desirous of carrying onward the effective welfare of Zion, by contributing to aid its children, again to renew the building of its walls. Mrs. Meshullam, especially, desires to be kindly remembered to you, and as a sister in the Lord, truly sympathizes with your difficulties; she, however, rejoices at the proposed prospect of seeing you again in this city, not failing to prize such truly Christian friendship. Do not fail to write, and command me, in any way, by which I may prove serviceable to you; and I trust, the next occasion to enlarge on the subject of your devoted interest. Believe us, your sincere friends.

JOHN MESHULLAM.

ARTOS, August 21st, 1850.

Beloved Christian Friend.—I beg to acknowledge the receipt of your letter, by which I am led to expect a beneficial result to my agricultural undertaking. It gave me great concern, that your letter arrived in an ill condition, through the various quarantine offices it passed, that I was unable fully to comprehend its contents. Although at first sight, I gathered sufficient cause to convince me, that you are prompted by no other than Christian beneficence, in contriving to promote this enterprise, for which I never cease to beg the Almighty to recompense you and your dear conjoiners abundantly. Before I pass on, to name the various hindrances and perplexities, I have recently met in my humble efforts to promote the good of this land, I feel dutifully bound to mention first, my unlimited thanks for the influence you have so disinterestedly exerted to lead other benefactors of Israel to favor, and contribute towards the approaching restoration of Zion. To such loving friends, I would quote the most appropriate passage of Scripture, "They shall prosper that love thee." My confidence in the Lord's promise of restoring his people, has increased to such a pitch of reliance, that quick as may be this decision, I am, through your instrumental influence, humbly led to concentrate my business to this point, with hopes furthered by Christian sympathy, to secure success. But to my correspondence. After having spent the half of last winter under a tent, and finding it impracticable for me and the serviceable animals for my agriculture to go on in such a position, I proceeded to rear four rooms, as circumstances permitted, at the lower end of the valley, economizing my labor by means of the adjoining rocks. Having taken such an important decision. I found it indispensably necessary to form habitations conducive to that health and comfort, of which, as Europeans, we felt in need, especially while removing my family to such a retired situation. Thus, since your departure, I have been enabled to build these rooms of sufficient extent, to hold my family and productions, which was aided by the rocky excavation forming the right angular portion of the building. At a little distance is situated a large stall, for the protection of my oxen, sheep, and other domestic animals, presenting in all a view, to recall a reverential reminiscence of the golden age of our patriarchal forefathers, comprising also, the tract of land which I occupy. I am happy to inform you, that addicting myself and family to necessity's call, and taking a retrospect of my past cares and persecutions, I am led to hope that they may here enjoy more peaceful and better days. Acceptable as this information may be to you, and those conjoined friends, who are desirous to promote Zion's welfare, it has not been received as such by sectarian opinions here, who when informed of my intention of removing my family to Artos, protested against the precarious positions to which I voluntarily exposed myself, as a responsible agent for living in a solitary valley, encircled by seven savage and barbarous tribes. This is, indeed, the real fact; but God, the supporter, and help of his people, has mercifully condescended to employ my reason, in leading these uncivilized people to view in me, and also to daily confess, a superior and benefactor. Thus difficulties have appeared seemingly to triumph, and drown those cultivated hopes, which only your kind and friendly correspondence has hitherto kept alive. Discouraged, as truly might have been, the most persevering mind, I verily confided in that Providence, who, while winking at the intricate machinations of men to oppose, says to the poor, "I will never leave thee, nor forsake thee." Such, dear friend, is the present state of things; blessings shall indeed rest on all those who favor Zion, and who amply seize the present favorable opportunity to rebuild its walls. * * * * * Respecting the mill, and various other articles which you and the good intentions of friends have contributed to send me, they will be received with the utmost acknowledgment of my unfeigned thanks. * * * * * As to your recommending me to employ Jews, I am truly concerned to say, that my present insignificant means will not allow me to admit the applications which they make. One great difficulty in which I am at present involved, (by removing his children from school in Jerusalem,) and that a vacancy, which can only be filled by the kind interest of friends, is to send a person, not only devoted to your correspondence, but also to be useful in promoting the education of my little children, which will be the only medium of counteracting the critical remarks of well disposed sectarians. * * * * * These considerations, I beg to transmit to you, and all Christian friends, who are interested in the behalf of an Israelite, whose prayer is, that "THE LORD MAY SEND FORTH LABORERS INTO HIS VINEYARD." Begging an immediate answer, allow me to inclose mine, and all my family's dutiful respect to you, in hope that we shall again meet, to share the productions of our own land.

Believe me, dear friend, your humble servant,

JOHN MESHULLAM.

The following is an extract from a letter, written by a German soon after his arrival in Palestine. It was publish by the *Rhenish Westphalian Jews' Society*, and contains a detailed account of Mr. Meshullam's gardens and farm in the Valley of Bethlehem, and of the rapid improvement of the general state of things in that land.

It seems by his testimony, that he arrived in the winter, a few months after we left Jerusalem; and that he at once joined the young man, that we have mentioned in the preceding journal, who commenced to labor in Meshullam's employ, in October, 1849. He does not publish his own name, or that of Meshullam, of whom he speaks, as a baptised and converted Jew, with whom they were conjointly engaged.

We learn by a letter from Mr. M. that after these German friends had labored with him awhile, and became acquainted with his manner of irrigation, and adaptation of the frequent crops, to the soil and climate, they were anxious to extend their operations, and took land of the neighboring Arabs, (to whom M. had at first restored their forfeited right,) in another part of the valley, where they are now happily improving the soil.

"We arrived in health and safety in Jerusalem, and went of course to the Brethren's House, where we were received with great kindness. We found employment almost immediately. Moller and John found work in their trades (as mason and joiner,) and Steinborn became a laborer. Gustav and his wife were appointed to the New English Churchyard, where they have a large fine garden, free lodgings, and a considerable annual income, 75 dollars (£11.) An excellent young man from Alsace, who was formerly in the Brethren's House in Jerusalem, settled half a year ago in Artos, near Bethlehem, in the gardens of Solomon, in the midst of Arabs. Conjointly with a baptized Jew in Jerusalem, he has farmed several of the gardens, and some land. They have also built a house there, although no good was prophesied for them; even the dear Bishop Gobat thought the undertaking too hazardous; but they have prospered beyond expectation. I at once joined this worthy young man. At first, before we had got properly into order, we found the weather anything but inviting, as it is frequently rainy and cold. But now, in the pleasant spring, when everything looks fresh and blooming, we find the locality most agreeable. I have erected my tent and use it both by day and night, Steinborn and his wife have also joined us here. We have already two cows and intend to purchase some more."

"This much we have already gained; all our neighbors, who are Turks, are well disposed towards us. We have also several friends in Bethlehem, where Christians and Turks live in good neighborhood. We can leave our house open by day and night without fear; as yet nothing has ever been purloined. In the beginning we had sometimes to be absent for three days together in Jerusalem; the house was left open, and entrusted to the Arabs; but even then we lost nothing."

"Moller has now also joined us at Artos. Stables are being erected for the cattle. We expect to earn our livelihood comfortably. No one of us desires to return. God turns his face again in mercy to this country. The abundant rain of the two last years, has again opened springs where for many years there were none, and also the pools of Solomon are full to overflowing. There are three, one above the other, and each so large and deep, that the largest steamboat might venture on it. The aqueduct constructed by Solomon from thence, via Bethlehem, to Jerusalem, is now beiug repaired. A Frenchman has sent mulberry seeds. As soon as our prospects shall have yet further improved, colonists from Wurtemberg and Alsace purpose settling here. There have now for two years been four men here, deputed by them, with the same object as brought us here. They have written home that people of property need not hesitate to come, as there is as much security here as in any other country, probably. But poor people would meet with some difficulties."

"An Arab works here for 3 sgr. (3¾*d.*) finding his own food; but joiners and masons earn 20 sgr. (2*s.*) Food is extremely cheap, especially flour, figs, eggs, rice, &c. With regard to larger colonies, a locality near the sea is to be preferred, with a view to exports. Twelve bushels of wheat cost in the market less than two Prussian dollars (6*d.*); and the peasants have perhaps to sit a whole day in the market, before they can sell so much. A pound of potatoes, however, cost in Jerusalem often 2 sgr. (2⅛*d.*) and at the present time, for instance, none at all can be had. Vegetables, likewise onions, carrots, beans, peas, celery, turnips, &c., are at times very dear. The country round Jerusalem is said to be the most unfruitful part of Palestine, and yet barley and wheat grow luxuriantly in the wretchedly cultivated soil, without any manure. The harrow and roller are unknown; the light plough in use here only rakes up a very little of the soil. On fruit land, which is not irrigated, comparatively few weeds grow. I have not yet seen the dangerous quick grass; but have noticed ten different kinds of clover, which grow wild in our gardens and on the mountains. I have planted in a corner six descriptions of the latter, and am laughed at for planting weeds. From this you will be able to conclude, how well adapted the soil is for agriculture, and rearing of catte."

"I have eleven bee-hives in Bethlehem. The bees are somewhat smaller than in Germany, and their color is a greyish yellow, but their qualities are not different. The fine weather and heavy dew, and the multitude of flowers and blossoms, lead us to calculate on a rich harvest, if they are properly tended, and God gives his blessing. If, therefore, you have a mind to visit us in spirit, you will, after having come from Jerusalem to Bethlehem, past the grave of Rachael and the well of Elijah, through fig and olive gardens and vineyards, until you arrive in our beautiful valley, find Moller employed on Masonry, Steinborn in digging, his wife in making butter, and myself, perhaps in milking—as I am the best hand at the latter, it becomes part of my occupation. Is it not sweet to have to do with milk and honey in the Holy Land!"

"But still we have many difficulties to encounter If we were but masters of the language, we should get on much better. But it is true that the emigration of single families is not advisable. The ice must, however, be broken by some one. Last year there were also two deputies here from America. In that country it is proposed to establish here a colony of twelve families, for the benefit of the Jews. In my opinion the question as to the possession of money is of greater importance than the number of families. As soon as the Arabs discover that they can derive profit from new comers, they suffer them willingly to dwell among them. They are well aware that the soil becomes more productive to them when farmed by us, than when cultivated by themselves; and, therefore, they readily leave us undisturbed. I have now rented garden land to the amount of forty-five dollars, in order to make a fair trial of what the soil can produce with proper cultivation. As yet no spade has been used; in consequence of the constant irrigation, the soil has become too solid, and the wretched plough has only raked it up for a few inches. Oats grow spontaneously everywhere, in the gardens and on the mountains. I counted thirty ears sprouting out of one corn; of barley, twenty. Barley and rye, also, frequently grow wild. I have not yet met with buckwheat and rapeseed. Among plants peculiar to the country, there is a kind of oil fruit, from which good sweet oil and lamp oil can be prepared. The Turkish wheat is roasted over charcoal, and is excellent if you have once got used to the taste."

"Fruit is abundant as oranges, olives, paradise apples, pome granates, &c. Beautiful dried figs are bought at ½*d.* or ¾*d.* the pound. There are at least forty gardens close to ours, in which there are above 1000 fig, peach, pomegranate, and pear trees. The valley, which is on both sides enclosed between high mountains, extends a distance of four hours' journey from the pools of Solomon to the Dead Sea. There are several opportunities for purchasing land; but as we do not yet know what may be our final destination, we defer making any purchase. I shall, however, soon get a flock of sheep, as the pasturage is every where free, and the flock can be removed, if we leave. There is, also, every facility for keeping goats, and you may have as many as you like."

"The heat is not excessive, and at present, a week after Easter, it is on rainy days still somewhat cold. When we arrived in Jerusalem, the snow lay pretty deep, and at times there was a sharp frost. A very mild winter in Germany is similar to the temperature here this year, except that the winter here is much shorter. As yet we have not found the sun too hot, and we find the climate in general extremely pleasant and healthy. My own relative, and Gustav, especially, look more full and healthy than ever; the children, also, thrive excellently. Whoever can be satisfied, as the country people here are, with bread, meal, eggs, oil, and milk, will find the living here both wholesome and cheap. But a person of many wants must bring a large supply of money, and even then, perhaps, he may not get on. Artizans of every kind are to be found in Jerusalem, where they are able to earn their livelihood. New comers, however, would have to struggle with difficulties before they can establish themselves in business. I can, therefore advise no one to come, unless an entire colony comes to settle here.

"Let, therefore, those who have at heart the well-being of this country and its people, promote the work as far as they are able, and rejoice in hope with us over Jerusalem, and the glorious promises relating to this country, such as Is. lxvi; li. 3, 11, &c.; Jer. xxxi: Ezek. xxxvi.: Joel, ii.; Amos. ix. 11, &c.; Micah vii. 20; Zeph. 3, 9, &c.; Zech. ii, 8, 14; Mal. iii. 16, &c. Many of these most precious promises begin already to be fulfilled; and who can continue to doubt when we behold with our own eyes the zeal of the whole world to bring succor to this country? From England, France, Germany, and Russia, there are parties here for the same purpose. America does not lag behind. A princess of the Netherlands remained lately above three months in this country. We long with much anxiety when the fulness of the Gentiles shall have come in, and so all Israel shall be saved. (Rom. xi. 25, 26.) When believing Israelites shall be named priests of the Lord, and ministers of our God. (Is. lxi. 5, 6.) We shall consider ourselves greatly honored in being permitted to be the ploughmen and vine-dressers. Until that time arrives, may God supply us with courage and power, that we may not carry on his work negligently, or suffer ourselves to be intimidated by difficulties."

"We consider the line of coast between Carmel and Jaffa, as proposed by Mr. Consul Weber, of Beyroot, best adapted for the establishment of a colony. The four brethren from Wurtemburg and Alsace, have, also, formerly travelled over the whole country, and not found a better spot for the purpose. There are still wells there, also sundry vaults, which would furnish shelter at the first commencement; a considerable quantity of wood and a fertile soil. If the undertaking be but once set on foot, the colony would soon receive additions from Wurtemburg and Alsace. But let every one who resolves to go out, carefully calculate the cost beforehand."

"I have observed, especially among the newly arrived colonists in Smyrna (where, however, everything was pretty well prepared for them,) that the women are exposed to many inconveniences, especially at the commencement of their residence here. Most women are probably, when the plan is first started, not very willing to leave home. The husband persuades the wife, represents the matter to her in the most favorable light, until, she, on her part, can hardly await the time for departure. If now even the journey has its hardships, and after their arrival many wants go unsatisfied, the wife not unfrequently reproaches her husband, as the people of Israel did Moses in the desert, when they said:—"Were there no graves in Egypt?" or, "there we sat by the flesh pots." I know very well that there are many good souls, like Mary of old, who in silent devotion thankfully accept all as from the hand of their Savior. But in a colony of 500, or even of but fifty families, there will always be some like the wives of Tobias and of Job. Young and newly married husbandmen, and such as have been accustomed to a life of much work and care, will succeed best in the struggle of first starting. I would rather begin in the most unfavorable spot with a few families, than with a large number in the very best locality, as in the latter case you must expect discontent and dissension. Money must however, on no account be wanting."

"We find, in general, that God gives to each country its advantages, as well as its disadvantages. But as in Holy Scripture this country is called pre-eminently a *good* one. It surely must, also, in reality be a *good* one."

Last autumn, Dr. P——, of this city, in concert with a German brother, who once resided three years in Jerusalem, mostly as teacher in Bishop Alexander's family, (the present Bishop Gobat's predecessor,) wrote to the believing brethren in Germany, respecting our proposed effort for the good of Israel in the holy land. An answer has been received, a translation of which he has kindly given, from which we make the following extracts, confirming the fact of a general and increasing interest, among the widely scattered people of God, in "THE PLACE OF THE NAME OF THE LORD OF HOSTS."

SHALLHUTTE, COUNTY OF BECKMANG, WURTEMBERG, January 2 1851.

"*Dear and esteeemed friend in Christ:*—To me also, teacher in this place, and one of the least of the brethren in Christ was your interesting letter sent, by the Christian brethren of Oberndorf and Rudersburg, that I might also get acquainted with your efforts for Palestine, as I am of the same opinion as themselves, about the hopes and promises to Israel and his land. * * * Not only expecting the glorious Advent, but believing the precious time predicted quite near, especially as we have lived to see the year 1848, and its events, and consequences. I see plainly that your ideas are grounded on the word of God, and also sent your letter to Fellback where brother K. is well known, and where a great number of Michael Hahn's brethren reside (a celebrated teacher of the coming and kingdom of God.)"

"Inclosed I send a letter of Prof. Paulus, who is director of a scientific institute, a school for Evangelists of the inner mission His views and labors incline to those of the old Moravians, while we hold the confession of Luther, at present we are the despised ones, and when the next revolution, that now already glimmers under the ashes of the former, shall break out, we shall have our lot with the persecuted ones. Respecting your letter I would repeat that we hold similar views with yourself, and it would afford us great pleasure, if we knew of any way to further your expectations. We have thus far acted according to the grace given and assure you, that we will in future, with our whole mind, take into serious consideration what you propose to us. We all greet you, and wish you many blessings, and hope you will make farther communications to us. Benigmus and Endrus, send their special love to brother K. Receive the greeting and love of the brethren of Orberndorf, Rudersberg, Schlechtbach, Winersden and Fellback. I remain your brother in the Lord."

G. M. REBER, *Teacher.*

We here add a large extract from the letter of Professor Paulus:

SALON, December 18, 1850.

Beloved Brethren in the Lord.—Grace be with you from Him which is, and which was, and which is to COME, our Lord Jesus Christ. We have read your dear letter with great interest and were convinced from it, that we are united with you in the bonds of the same spirit, which gave us all great joy. For we too like yourself are convinced with lively hope, that the coming of the Lord is not only nigh at hand, but also, that the promised land in connection with this truth, will have to act a conspicuous part, and from time to time, we feel the drawings of our hearts more distinctly directed towards that land, yet we have not arrived at the joyful resolve to go, and know not for what the Lord will keep us here, but stand in His service waiting for His orders. Some years since, our countryman, C. F. Spittler, in Basle was convinced that the Holy Land should be occupied by "Believers," and to that end he sent brethren, and established and maintains a house in Jerusalem,* which forms as it were an outpost in Palestine, but thus far the result of their labors, has not encouraged us, that the time had arrived to go *en masse* with our families to locate there. (The writer had not heard of these brethren's later success with Meshullam.) A year ago some Hessian brethren desiring to emigrate to the Holy Land in large numbers, wrote to Bishop Gobat for his opinion. But his advice was against the undertaking saying "the time for such a scheme has not yet arrived." Since this answer all is silent again, and we stand, with regard to this cause, like servants waiting for the sign, and order of their Master. But by no means, by these statements, would we discourage you, but we would rather say go on, to labor in this cause, and whosoever feels free and convinced to emigrate to the land of our hope, let him go in God's name, and God in whom he trusts will surely

* The young man who commenced to labor with Meshullam in Oct. 1849, was one of the four then residing together in Jerusalem.

not let him be confounded. We are convinced that the time HAS ARRIVED, when the Lord will prepare habitations for his people, in that land (Ez. 368) which has seen him onee in humiliation, but will soon see him also in exaltation and glory."

"We farther believe, that the promised land, will now become a point, or object, with which believers will have more work to DO, than heretofore. To assist in spirit, and by prayer, and if necessary to help with our substance, we will do cheerfully; and will rejoice if one here and there feels moved to get up and proceed to that land. We also believe that the Lord has ALREADY singled out such of his people, whom he will use in PREPARING the place of his Advent"

"We beg leave thus to lay our hearts open to God, and rejoice, that we have made your brotherly acquaintance, though only by letter, the communion and friendship in Christ is so sweet and elevating, that we feel strengthened in thankfulness to the Lord. Heartily would we rejoice to hear from you of the progress of the work, in which seemingly the Lord has called you, that we may rejoice with you, and pray the more earnestly, for the work, even if we cannot go with you in person, we commend you to God; the Lord be with you and bless your labor which is dedicated to Him with the richness of his mercy. I salute you with the kiss of love in behalf of all the brethren whom your letter has reached, and in spirit, I stretch my loving brother's hand over the ocean.

Yours united in the Lord. PH. PAULUS,

Director of the Scientific Institute, near Ludvigsburg.

Mr. Meshullam having given one of his German neighbors some of the medicine which was sent in our first shipment, (June, 1850,) and also given them the kind letter of the donor to read. Dr. P—— has just received a very interesting letter from his patient in Palestine, a translation of which he kindly furnishes for publication.

JERUSALEM, November 29, 1850.

Dear and Beloved Brother in the Lord.—Hearing of your faith and hope in the Lord Jesus, and of your love, toward the people of the old covenant, we were highly rejoiced, and that you in common with us, feel such a deep interest in seeing that the inheritance of the despised seed of Abraham, is again cultivated by believers. I was so fortunate, as to read your dear letter, to your friend Mr. Meshullam, which he gave me to peruse, so that I am enabled now to write to you, and give the beloved ones in America a few facts concerning us here. Who will not be exceedingly glad to hear the good tidings that the children of Zion, flock hither again, from the north, south, east, and west. Also, how others, who cannot see as we do, and who do not YET feel as we did HOMESICK for the Holy Land, how even these, begin to look with a wishful eye, towards the land of divine Revelation. We may count ourselves happy, to have lived to see these days, and manifestations, how the Lord HAS TURNED towards his land, and people, in grace and loving kindness, and has COMMENCED to chastise, LUKEWARM backsliden Christendom, and to let loose among them the evil spirits of rebellion and anarchy. But He will perform the truth to Jacob, and the mercy to Abraham, and He will smile again, upon the long forsaken and desolate widow Jerusalem. We came to this country nearly a year ago, from the Rhine province in Prussia, where are many brethren holding the same faith with us, about the restoration of Israel, and the coming of the Lord. Within THE LAST FEW YEARS, there were several societies established for Israel, and colporters sent out to the Jews, to distribute Bibles among them. Through these movements, many of us became so interested in behalf of the Holy Land, that many would willingly have started at once to emigrate there, if the undertaking had not seemed too hazardous at the present time.

We came to the conclusion, to raise some funds, and to send first two deputies to Palestine, in order to ascertain if it were possible for us to dwell there with our families. Unfortunately most of the brethren who felt interested were farmers and mechanics, who had suffered much THE LAST FEW YEARS, from the failure of the produce of the fields, war, etc., so that money was scarce. Now in order that the cause might not suffer by delay, and in order to find out soon, if it were practicable to live in peace among the Arabs, and gain bread sufficient for our families, we concluded at once to go there with our families. Our beloved father gave each of us, several hundred dollars, and after many blessings from our people, we left them on Nov. 29, '49 by railroad from Barmen."

"When we left, we numbered ten persons, five men, two women, and three children, the least of whom was two and a half years old. God Almighty brought us wonderfully through many storms, by sea and land, so we arrived after ten weeks, safely in Jerusalem! except one sister, who was confined in a village six hours from Jerusalem (Ramlah) where we stopped all night. She remained with the child and her husband until she was able to proceed, although she had no physician, and could not converse a word with the Arab women, who kindly waited on her, yet the Lord, interceded in such a manner, that on the fifth day she was able to proceed on her journey on horseback, (up the rocky ascent!) to Jerusalem! Having all arrived, we advised, and consulted with this and that person, about our future course, but generally they prophesied us no good. One gentleman thought "settling in the country is yet too insecure" another said, "thesoil is too unproductive" But trusting in God, we were not discouraged, but gradually looked about at things as they were, and hired out as day laborers, and began to pick up a little of the language. After this we bought some cows, sheep, and goats. We had brought with us some good churns, by means of which our butter very soon proved quite a celebrated object in Jerusalem, which we sold at a good price in the season of English and other travellers. The Arabs prepare their butter in goat skins, and are not very nice in in their mode of doing things. We have two large gardens, in which we plant European vegetables, etc., which we sell to the city. Thus we have worked our way thus far by God's blessing. To live among the Turks is easy enough, if we know a little of their language, on the other hand there is of course some difficulties to encounter. In keeping cattle there is something to be learned by a new comer, as the nature of the animals, as well as the climate is different from other countries. We have now five cows and five calves a year old, two horses and one foal, and we are convinced that the raising of live stock is as profitable now, as it was in the time of Father Abraham, for the pasture is plenty, and free for all! It is probable that some wealthy merchants will soon locate near Jaffa where they have BOUGHT some gardens, and intend to rear the silk worm, as mulberry trees abound there, and some good beginning has already been made. We are happy to state that since our arrival, we have all been indeed very happy, and not a single moment has any one of us regretted coming to live here. This fall when I had the chills and fever, and was cured by one portion (a few doses) of your medicine, and herewith I would tender you my most heartfelt thanks for your kind provident care. Mr. Meshullam and family are all quite well, we all send you affectionate regards, and I remain your brother in Christ."

FREDERICK GROSSTEINSBECK.

P. S.—Please to write to us and I will make farther communications about our doings here.

The following is our most recent intelligence from Mr. Meshullam, and contains his acknowledgment of the first shipment of last June, comprising the mill and accompanying donations.

JERUSALEM, November 26, 1850.

Beloved Christian Friend:—Influenced by motives of regard and gratitude I beg to send the following acknowledgement of your letter of June, in which I felt deeply impressed, with a feeling of mutual esteem, being again called upon to view your disinterested love, and extended efforts to promote so charitable a cause. I inscribe my humble appreciation, and heartfelt thanks for the articles recently received, particularly, as they convey an insight into the minds of those persons, who by such benevolence, express a peculiar love, and desire, to further the cause of God's chosen people."

First of all, I would undersign my acknowledgement of the mill, and all the various accompanying articles, contributed to extend my labors, in the position assigned me by Providence."

"The criterion by which my gratitude is to be proved in return, remains in the reciprocal purpose, and congenial feelings of my heart. If the Lord is indeed supporting my undertaking, in behalf of his afflicted people, He will I am sure, finish the work He has begun, and make me in future the instrument of His purpose, but if otherwise, I simply commit to his Providence, the care of my personal concern in it. We fully appreciate that your intended return, is only proposed from motives of Christian interest, and we embrace the welcome hour, that shall convey you safe to our improved cot, at Artos. Many are the evident, and increasing tokens, that the Lord's eyes are turned for good, on Jacob's heritage. Let but Islamism flee from our strong holds and the Lord's purpose find room, amid the the broken fragments of this desolate land, and the FIRST STEP of civilization, and industrial labor, in cultivation SPREAD among the vallies of Palestine, and find its way, effectually to Jewish quarters, then in the due and predicted time, the Lord will appear and openly exhibit the majestic band that is to return to Zion, and his hand shall dry up Israel's tears, when a remnant shall come out from the furnace of long affliction, as pure as the native gold of ancient Armenia. With these approaching prospects in view permit me to close, with my unfeigned thanks for all the kind interest you have exerted on my behalf, trusting that the most acceptable answer to these lines may be, your own personal conveyance to my house and farm. In conclusion dear friends, we all desire to be dutifully remembered to you and all other Christian friends connected with you in the Lord, in the fervent hope, to meet again with unparting prospects. Believe me, yours faithfully.

JOHN MESHULLAM.

P. S.—Permit me to mention about the mill, having read in your letter, that it was capable of grinding two barrels of flour per hour (with horse power) I promised a number of poor Jews, and Gentiles, to allow them to grind if they would pray for the remuneration of its contributors, and to begin to pray in advance, for alleviating them from so great a fatigue and expense. So, many poor people came to grind a little wheat, for their own poor families, but they were not able to succeed, for on account of the great suffering of the people in this country, their power is much fallen, and for ten minutes they can resist grinding, but no longer. Now to these poor people it seems so hard in me, after having promised them to tell them it is too difficult to grind, they being unwilling to believe it. The things necessary to apply horse power, I am sorry to say, are not to be obtained here. I shall feel greatly obliged if you can give me any advice, to make it grind easier.

Please to inform Dr. P. that there are many blessings for him, from several individuals, on whom his medicine had great effect, not being able to write to him, as I am much occupied with the land."

J. M.

A few words were added from Mrs. Meshullam:

"I take the opportunity of sending a few lines in order to express my hearty thanks, for your kind undertaking for me and my family, since your departure, and hoping that your intention is to return, to this land, I can only pray that the Lord may bring you safe to it and that we may all be united in one family in Christ Jesus. My best respects to all other kind friends connected with you."

Yours truly,

MARY MESHULLAM.

Elijah, the eldest son, writes a business letter, containing a list of tools and implements which he needs, but cannot be obtained there, he says:

JERUSALEM, January, 1850.

"Permit to me close, with mine and my parents best love to you. Artos is still FLOURISHING and under the divine blessing, every thing is ready to receive you. With our united love and prayer believe me, yours faithfully and obediently."

ELIJAH MESHULLAM.

PHILADELPHIA, April 11, 1851.

On account of an unexpected delay in the press, we are able to add the following letter from Mr. Meshullam, this day received, in an unusual short time. The mail steamer leaves Jaffa on the 3d of every month, so that it has reached us in 40 days from Palestine. The surprising intelligence of such abundant rains, increases our confidence that "the set time" to favor the desolations of Zion is truly come, when the Lord has promised, "fear not, O Jacob, my servant, and thou Jeshuran, whom I have chosen, for I will POUR water upon him that is thirsty, and FLOODS upon the dry ground," "and waters in the wilderness, and rivers in the desert, to give drink to MY people, my chosen."

"CHARLES A. MINOR, No. 141 Spruce Street, Philadelphia, United States."

JERUSALEM, February 27, 1851.

"BELOVED CHRISTIAN FRIEND:—I was exceedingly happy to receive your worthy letter, dated January 5th, 1851, in which I observed that my final settlement at Artos caused great satisfaction to you and your Christian friends As you have decided to come, allow me to describe to you the present state of things in this place, which I believe you will be anxious to hear. The additional land which I occupy this year, lies between Artos and the ruin called the House of the Prophet Zachariah, and consists of about 50 acres of land, or 72 days ploughing, (with the poor Arab plough.) If the Lord should bless the soil, and allow me an abundant harvest, I shall divide it in three parts, namely: one-third to the two German families, having a contract with them until November, and four Arabs, annual laborers; one-third to the POOR, and a third to the support of my family, which I am able to get, yet not without persecution. To this, I submit, knowing that every good Christian must suffer more or less in this country, and our recompense is not in this world, but in the world to come, having no defence but prayer and supplication to the Lord. Whoever can submit to these terms, are welcome to unite with us, giving you information that the land is not entirely mine, having one portion of it for the period of ten years, and the rest has been given into my hands to cultivate for the benefit of the poor; the Mahomedans here, trusting more to my faith, than to that of their own nation, so that the benefit is not only for myself, but for others. While I beg you to consider, to what we are subject, I would repeat once more, that THE OBJECT of my agricultural undertaking, in this desolate place, among mountains and rocks, is to LAY A FOUNDATION for my brethren to take an example of cultivating their Father-land. I hope the Lord will inspire them, and show them that man should not fear for MAN, but only for the LORD, for he will be with us, even among these desolate places, if we accomplish his will, and our duty—to labor for an honest living.

I was not less rejoiced than yourself to receive your recent communication, for though I dwell under my own vine and fig tree, Satan often thwarts, through hostile influences, my ONE OBJECT of LOVE and beneficence. You speak of Mr. —— opposition; if there should be any who desire to have further information respecting me, I would refer them to my friend, Bishop Gobat, of Jerusalem, Rev. J. Nicolayson, Chaplain, and Dr. Magowan, of the Medical Department. I should inform you, that during this rainy season, we received three days and three nights of such great rain, that it destroyed nearly a third of the walls and houses of Jerusalem! I was also a sufferer, as my farm was completely covered with water, from one side of the mountain to the other, (it occupies a narrow valley between two high ranges of naked rocks.) The water was about ten times the usual depth of the Jordan, on which vessels could navigate, it lasting for more than two months!! I lost all my winter vegetables, and my four rooms were nearly destroyed, so that all my laborers were obliged to flee to the top of the mountains, in order to escape being drowned. The damage in all was about £140. The oldest men in Palestine, declare they have never seen such rain during their lives! I and my family were happily in the city during that weather. I shall be greatly obliged to you, if you will thank Mrs. E. D. R. with many thanks, for the £10 forwarded by her, and received this day, and I trust she will be pleased with my distribution, among those whom I know to be in the most need while cultivating the land, they begging me to send their earnest blessing for her. I also acknowledge again the mill, and all the other accompanying articles. It will be necessary for you to bring with you a quantity of thick oil cloth, or canvass, well waxed, or tarred, being more secure from DEW and RAINS than common tents. Light stoves or portable furnaces for the winter, strong cloths for bags, buckets for drawing and for carrying water, and a small engine or pump. Seeds of all descriptions, mostly beet roots, turnips, aud cabbages. Horse radish is especially much admired by the Jews, as they suppose it capable of curing them from any disease; also, implements and tools of all descriptions. The above things being the most requisite in this country. Excuse me, having no more time to write, as the post is leaving. Our best Christian Love to you all. I remain yours, most truly, in the Lord."

JOHN MESHULLAM.

RECEIPTS AND EXPENDITURES.

RECEIPTS.

Account of the receipt of money and donations of different articles received, for the purpose of aiding the benevolent labors of John Meshullam, and "the Manual Labor School of Agriculture for the Jews in the Holy Land:"

April 4, 1850—Received the first dollar from a poor widow, on board the steamer from Southampton, . $1 00
May—From a lady in Philadelphia, through E. D. R. . 25 00
" an Association of ladies, do. . . 20 00
" a lady, do. . . . 10 00
" " a friend of the Jews, do. . . 55 00
" the same, two pieces of gingham.
June: " a believing brother, ... 5 00
A box of flower seeds from two sisters.
A box of medicine from a physician.
Several articles of children's clothing, from his lady.
From a lady in Spruce St. 2 dress patterns of gingham.
" a florist, and agricultnral book.
" a lady, 2 Marseilles quilt vests, and a worsted scarf.
Several tools and appliances for the Mill, by the patentee.
Aug.—Through a friend at the sea shore, from a Scotch lady, 5 00
From another, to pay one laborer, one month, . 5 50
Oct.—From a lady in Philadelphia, by C. B. . . . 5 00
" Ladies' Mite Society, for a fanning mill, etc. through E. D. R. 24 00
Nov.—From a lady, ... 1 00
" " a lover of Israel, ... 42 00
" a lady, ... 1 00
" Farmersville Church, N. Y., by B. S. G. . . 5 00
Sale of Meshullam's Narrative, ... 5 00
By a lady, from various individuals, ... 6 70
By another, ... 2 50
1851, Jan.—From a "Friend," (E. P.) Maryland, . . 5 00
From the same, 1 keg of assorted seeds, another keg containing dried peaches and apples, six brooms, best quality, and a bag of hops.
From another "Friend" in Maryland, 1 new patch work bed quilt, a superior article.
From a lady in Spruce Street, 1 dress pattern of calico, and 1 of mourning lawn.

Feb.—From A. B. W. through Dr. P., ... 2 00
" a Presbyterian Clergyman, Philadelphia, . 1 00
" B. P. a brown linen dress.
" J. W. a boy's cloth cap.
" 27—From N. B. A. & Co., New York, a donation of agri cultural implements, ... 32 94

Total, ... $256 64
Money remaining in the hands of the agent, . 10 70
Also, a few of the articles named in the receipt, to be sent in the next shipment; also, five dollars and thirty cents, contributed by personal friends, in N. Y., for our contingent expenses.

EXPENDITURES.

Account of monies expended, and appropriations of donations received:

June, 1850: Shipped from Philadelphia, through the kindness of Dr. J. P. R. of England, to John Meshullam, Jerusalem.

One large box, containing a portable burr-stone flour mill, which cost, ... $50 00
Also, necessary implements, bolters, etc. 8 00
Another box, containing seeds, dry goods, clothing, medicine, etc., from individuals, embracing all the articles received at that date.
Also, a package of choice garden seeds and 2 hoes, . 5 00
Two bills of exchange, for fifty dollars each, . 100 00
Was also forwarded by E. D. R. through the Christian courtesy of Mr. B. W. N. of London, to John Meshullam, to aid his benevolent efforts in behalf of his poor brethren.

March 1, 1851: Three large boxes were shipped from New York, to the care of the American Consul, Beyroot, for John Meshullam. They contained agricultural implements, books and seeds, according to the desire of the donors, and the greatest need of the farm in the valley of Bethlehem. The following is a list of the articles contained in the boxes, with their prices:

Bought of N. B. A. & Co., N. Y., Feb. 26, 1851:

1 plough, No. 18, $3 25; 1 plough, No. 4, $3 25; 1 fanning mill, No. 1, $13; 1 frame and pulley wheel, and leathern belt, to increase the power, and apply to the mill, already sent, $15; 1 ox chain, 14 lbs. $1 75; 1 sickle, 50 cts.; 1 small corn mill, $6 50,—very easy to grind; 6 garden hoes, $3; 1 rake, 37 cts.; 4 assorted hoes, $1 75; 1 shovel and spade, $1 75; other assorted samples of farming implements, $7 12,

garden seeds, $5 14; extra boxing and cartage, $6. Also, after a liberal discount from our generous FRIEND, Capt. H., paid for freight from New York to Beyroot, $10; amounting in all, by cash paid, $50; and the gratuity of N. B. A. & Co., $32 94, . $82 94

Total amount sent, ... $245 94

ACCOUNT OF PRINTING.

Money contributed to print the first edition of Meshullam's Narrative:

May, 1850:	A lady in Philadelphia,	$10 00
	Another do.	5 00
	A friend,	1 00
	A lady,	50
	Another,	50
	A lady,	2 50
		$19 50
June:	Paid the printer, in full, for 1,000 copies of M's Narrative,	$22 00

Account of money received to aid in the publication of the first edition of this work, containing the Journal, and second edition of Meshullam's Narrative:

Jan. 1851:	From a friend, a lady of Philadelphia,	$20 00
	A poor widow,	75
	An advent sister,	50
	A lady in Spruce Street,	1 00
	An orphan child,	25
	An advent brother,	1 00
	Another,	1 50
	A lady,	5 00
	A sick lad, a tithe of Christmas money,	50
	A lady in Arch Street,	10 00
		$40 50
	Paid for printing and binding 1,000 copies of "Meshullam, or Tidings from Jerusalem,"	$123 35
March 25:	Received for the sale of "the Tidings from Jerusalem,"	60 21
	Deduction for postage and advertising,	4 24
		$55 97

CHARLES A. MINOR, *Agent.*

PHILADELPHIA, *March* 27, 1851.

APPEAL.

PHILADELPHIA, *April* 1, 1851.

The first edition of this work being exhausted, and application for copies and the interest in its subject still increasing, a disinterested conviction of duty, and dèvotion to the *hope* of Israel, has constrained me to re-publish it. Since our return from Jerusalem, we have communicated with many intelligent Christians in different parts of this country, who agree in prayer and faith in this interesting work of love. Some have generously contributed, and their free-will offering has been sent, to this altar of service, which the Lord is rearing again, amid the ashes of Zion!

Meshullam, in recent letters, still appeals for *helpers* in humble labor, and this "cry from Jerusalem," deserves a serious response from those who have long professed to be lovers of Israel. Having, by personal observation, and careful inquiry from others, ascertained these facts respecting his character, and investigated his present position and relations to the inhabitants of the country, and his Jewish brethren, the conviction is pressing upon us, that the Lord is preparing and sustaining him, not as a spiritual leader, but as an humble agent of usefulness, and hopeful blessing, to Israel. Also, that in accordance with this manifestation of the Divine Providence, a few humble laboring Christians, should immediately join, and co-operate with him, in something like a *Manual Labor School of Agriculture for the Jews.* The way for these unpretending labors seems to have been remarkably opened, the past year, in perfect harmony with other movements respecting Israel. Last summer an agent from Constantinople, arrived in the United States, confirming the most favorable relations, between our Government and the Sublime Porte; also, since our return from the East, the Sultan of Turkey has issued a Firman, giving permission to *all* denominations, to *build*, *own*, and *occupy* lands in Palestine! Also in a published letter from Constantinople, dated December, 1850, it is stated that a Firman had just been received by the Protestants of Turkey, from the Sublime Porte, and the writer adds: "By this Firman all the civil and religious rights of the Protestants are secured to them, and they are distinctly declared to have the privilege of building churches, holding burying grounds," etc. This is a liberty which has never before existed since the dispersion, and is surely an unexampled and dispensational movement of Providence. Also, another serious obstacle is removed, and the impracticability and expense greatly lessened, by the recent establishment of a line of sailing vessels, between our country and the land of Israel! The gentlemen in New York who sent the first merchant vessel to Syria, mentioned in the Journal for last year, (with whom we correspond,) have continued a line of communication, by which passengers, and freight, may be landed at Jaffa, at a reasonable charge! Pious, industrious laborers, are indispensable to the success of *this* benevolent work, as the labor is too great for one, however intelligent and devoted, for the poor Jews must be taught, not only by precept, but by daily example, the first strokes of successful tillage. A few such humble laborers for the love of Christ, have submitted themselves to the Lord, as candidates for this arduous service of self-denial and sacrifice. They have for a long time, from a conscientious reverence for the fourth commandment, sanctified and kept the Sabbath of the Lord, (the Seventh day of the week,) though unconnected with any organized sect, and are thus peculiarly prepared to co-operate with the Jews in manual labor, without disarranging THIS vital point in their religion. IF the God of Israel should move the hearts of any of his Gentile children to have compassion upon HIS poor in Zion, and the means should be provided for the bare necessities of the voyage, and their first establishment, these laborers desire, at once, to proceed to the aid of Meshullam, where their first object will be to secure lands by perpetual lease, in concert with him, at a moderate expense. They must also be provided with a large supply of all kinds of useful seeds, agricultural tools, implements, and fixtures, and a small assortment of common mechanical tools, to meet the exigencies of a new residence in a destitute land. They will also need common dry groceries and provisions for the first few months; also, saddles and bridles, tents, and their furniture, etc. It will be also necessary that they should have a few coarse cotton goods, to clothe the destitute, and a small fund to employ the suffering applicants: but it must be distinctly understood, that they chiefly depend upon the fertility of the soil, and the blessing of God upon their labors, to sustain and extend this interesting work. Are there not servants of the Lord, scattered in all denominations and classes of society, who will desire a share in this labor, and be constrained, by the love of Christ, to send an offering to the Lord in Zion! If any such should respond to this humble APPEAL, their smallest contributions, in money, or any of the necessary articles mentioned above, will be faithfully and conscientiously appropriated AS THE DONORS SHALL SIGNIFY, to the immediate needs of this work.

Any communications, or donations, by letter or otherwise, "FOR THE MANUAL LABOR SCHOOL OF AGRICULTURE FOR THE JEWS IN THE HOLY LAND," may be addressed (*post-paid*,) to their Agent,

CHARLES A. MINOR,

"No. 141 Spruce street, above Fifth, Philadelphia," where this work is for sale.

www.ingramcontent.com/pod-product-compliance
Lightning Source LLC
LaVergne TN
LVHW021413110826
845150LV00007B/1910

* 9 7 8 1 4 2 5 5 1 0 3 2 9 *